Corinth. An exemplary book that should be read by all who seek to understand the gospel of Christ and to relate it to contemporary society."

—William S. Campbell
Reader in Biblical Studies, School of Theology, Religious Studies and Islamic Studies, University of Wales, Trinity Saint David

"Brian Tucker offers a new way to follow Paul's arguments throughout 1 Corinthians by deftly weaving together the usual methodologies employed in historical exegesis with a sustained focus on insights gained from social identity theory. Tucker's reading of the letter is clear and coherent."

—**Mark D. Nanos**
University of Kansas, author of *The Mystery of Romans*, *The Irony of Galatians*, and most recently, co-editor of *Paul within Judaism*

"This is no typical commentary on 1 Corinthians. Recognizing the importance of identity and with expertise in identity theory, Brian Tucker supplies an identity lens for readers to see with new perspective. The result is a practical and insightful explanation of 1 Corinthians which underscores how much Scripture focuses on identity issues and how relevant such thinking is for theological and missional purposes. This book deserves your attention."

—**Klyne Snodgrass**
Emeritus Professor of New Testament, North Park Theological Seminary, author of *Stories with Intent: A Comprehensive Guide to the Parables of Jesus*

"J. Brian Tucker's *Reading 1 Corinthians* offers students, pastors, and general readers a sustained commentary on Paul's most practical epistle through the generative lens of social identity theory. American readers will value Tucker's lucid summary of the theories of Henri Tajfel and John Turner on the construction of social identity. The application of social identity theory to 1 Corinthians is especially appropriate, since the multiplicity of issues dealt with in 1 Corinthians reflects the diverse social and ethnic makeup of the Christ groups at Corinth, and reveals the presence and influence of a group of strong-minded persons whose views on a variety of subjects diverged sharply from Paul's own. At every point, Tucker succeeds in communicating the relevance of Paul's project in constructing and transforming social identity in Christ for the complex ethical decisions facing readers today."

—L. L. Welborn
Professor of New Testament and Early Christianity, Fordham University

"By applying social identity theory from social psychology, Brian Tucker brilliantly re-situates and re-interprets all of the major questions raised by 1 Corinthians. While interacting with the best recent scholarship, the book is written succinctly and with a limpid style admirably attuned to the general audience at whom it is aimed. The astute discussion questions posed after each section show how easily within a social identity perspective Paul's ideas can be brought into fruitful dialogue with contemporary issues. If you only have time for one book on 1 Corinthians, choose this one."

—Philip F. Esler
Portland Chair in New Testament Studies in the University of Gloucestershire, Cheltenham, UK, author of *Babatha's Orchard: The Yadin Papyri and An Ancient Jewish Family Tale Retold* (2017) and the editor of *The Early Christian World*, second edition (2017).

"Tucker, in this post-supersessionist reading of 1 Corinthians, presents Paul as seeking to construct an identity of calling in which existing identities are not erased but transformed, and in which key aspects of Roman social and civic identity are not rejected but tempered in keeping with the call of God. A brilliant and original application of Social Identity Theory to a Pauline text that shows what Pauline transformation through the call of God meant for those in

READING
1 CORINTHIANS

CASCADE COMPANIONS

The Christian theological tradition provides an embarrassment of riches: from Scripture to modern scholarship, we are blessed with a vast and complex theological inheritance. And yet this feast of traditional riches is too frequently inaccessible to the general reader.

The Cascade Companions series addresses the challenge by publishing books that combine academic rigor with broad appeal and readability. They aim to introduce nonspecialist readers to that vital storehouse of authors, documents, themes, histories, arguments, and movements that comprise this heritage with brief yet compelling volumes.

TITLES IN THIS SERIES:

Reading Augustine by Jason Byassee
Conflict, Community, and Honor by John H. Elliott
An Introduction to the Desert Fathers by Jason Byassee
Reading Paul by Michael J. Gorman
Theology and Culture by D. Stephen Long
Creation and Evolution by Tatha Wiley
Theological Interpretation of Scripture by Stephen Fowl
Reading Bonhoeffer by Geffrey B. Kelly
Justpeace Ethics by Jarem Sawatsky
Feminism and Christianity by Caryn D. Griswold
Angels, Worms, and Bogeys by Michelle A. Clifton-Soderstrom
Christianity and Politics by C. C. Pecknold
A Way to Scholasticism by Peter S. Dillard
Theological Theodicy by Daniel Castelo
The Letter to the Hebrews in Social-Scientific Perspective
  by David A. deSilva
Basil of Caesarea by Andrew Radde-Galwitz
A Guide to St. Symeon the New Theologian by Hannah Hunt
Reading John by Christopher W. Skinner
Forgiveness by Anthony Bash
Jacob Arminius by Rustin Brian
Reading Jeremiah by Jack Lundbom
John Calvin by Donald McKim

READING
1 CORINTHIANS

J. BRIAN TUCKER

CASCADE *Books* • Eugene, Oregon

READING 1 CORINTHIANS

Cascade Companions

Copyright © 2017 J. Brian Tucker. All rights reserved. Except for brief quotations in critical publications or reviews, no part of this book may be reproduced in any manner without prior written permission from the publisher. Write: Permissions, Wipf and Stock Publishers, 199 W. 8th Ave., Suite 3, Eugene, OR 97401.

Cascade Books
An Imprint of Wipf and Stock Publishers
199 W. 8th Ave., Suite 3
Eugene, OR 97401

www.wipfandstock.com

PAPERBACK ISBN: 978-1-4982-9293-1
HARDCOVER ISBN: 978-1-4982-9295-5
EBOOK ISBN: 978-1-4982-9294-8

Cataloging-in-Publication data:

Names: Tucker, J. Brian

Title: Reading 1 Corinthians / by J. Brian Tucker.

Description: Eugene, OR : Cascade Books, 2017 | Series: Cascade Companions | Includes bibliographical references.

Identifiers: ISBN 978-1-4982-9293-1 (paperback) | ISBN 978-1-4982-9295-5 (hardcover) | ISBN 978-1-4982-9294-8 (ebook)

Subjects: LCSH: Bible. Corinthians, 1st—Social scientific criticism. | Bible. Corinthians, 1st—Criticism, interpretation, etc.

Classification: LCC BS2675.2 T8 2017 (print) | LCC BS2675.2 (ebook)

Manufactured in the U.S.A.   08/10/17

CONTENTS

Preface • vii

1 Introduction • 1
2 Reading 1 Corinthians • 11
3 Corinth and Its Roman Civic Identity • 24
4 "Be United in the Same Mind and the Same Purpose" (1:1—2:16) • 38
5 "You Belong to Christ" (3:1—4:21) • 54
6 "The Body for the Lord" (5:1—7:40) • 72
7 "Do Everything for the Glory of God" (8:1—11:1) • 88
8 "All Things Should Be Done Decently and in Order" (11:2—14:40) • 106
9 "Let All You Do Be Done in Love" (15:1—16:24) • 124
10 Conclusion • 141

Bibliography • 145

PREFACE

My interest in 1 Corinthians extends back to an undergraduate course taught by William A. Simmons where I saw for the first time the way this text could holistically inform one's life and practice. It continued on into my seminary studies and formed part of a Doctor of Ministry dissertation I wrote that addressed how to preach to the over-churched, based on 1 Corinthians 8–10. Not yet satisfied, I eventually wrote a PhD thesis at the University of Wales, Lampeter on the way 1 Corinthians 1–4 forms social identity. The book you are reading is based on my earlier works: *You Belong to Christ* and *Remain in Your Calling* and highlights many ideas that will be fully developed in my forthcoming large-scale commentary on the letter.[1] I hope that this present book will offer the reader an introduction to the current scholarship on this letter and a compelling post-supersessionist reading of it through the lens of social identity theory.

1. Tucker, *You Belong to Christ*; Tucker, *Remain in Your Calling*. Much of the contents of this book are developed more fully in these. They are academic and technical but provide a wealth of primary sources and theoretical information.

Preface

A couple of important points should be kept in mind. The outline that is given later in the book would allow for a manageable series of sermons or studies if one were interested in such an endeavor. While this structure is somewhat artificial, it does serve as an entry point and generally reflects the conclusions of some of the commentators on the letter. Throughout the book, I will offer definitions of many unfamiliar terms. These are framed for this particular study and should not be construed as precise scholarly definitions; rather, they are used for the practical purposes of reading 1 Corinthians. The end of each chapter contains several discussion questions. I have written them in the hopes that readers will think critically about their own context in light of the reading offered here.

This book was written during my 2016 sabbatical leave, and thus I owe a debt of gratitude to my colleagues and the administration of Moody Theological Seminary, especially John Jelinek and Larry Davidhizar, for helping make this sabbatical possible. I want to thank Matthew Novenson for inviting me as a guest of the Centre for the Study of Christian Origins at the University of Edinburgh (New College) and to Tom Breimaier for his hospitality and research assistance during my time in Edinburgh. The staff at the Greek Bible College in Athens, Greece, were particularly helpful during my time there, and Samuel Spatola, the Dean of the Saints Bible Institute in San Lorenzo, Italy, provided excellent support and interaction during my stay there. Thanks to the students in my 1 Corinthians class who raised provocative and insightful questions while going through earlier versions of this material. In particular, I want to thank Laura J. Hunt for her careful reading, suggestions, and editing of this book. Laura successfully defended her PhD thesis at the University of Wales Trinity Saint David during the final stages of this book and was gracious with

Preface

her time. Her 2011 book, *The Not-Very-Persecuted Church: Paul at the Intersection of Church and Culture*, would be a good next step for some of the ideas introduced in relation to 1 Corinthians 1–4 in this book.

I want to thank the staff at Cascade Books for their continued support. Chris Spinks provided encouragement and insight throughout the process while Christian Amondson offered the initial invitation and guidance for the inclusion of this book in the Cascade Companions series. Their combined comments and constructive suggestions have made this a much better work, though I realize I am responsible for all the shortcomings that remain. Thanks to those who discussed these ideas with me: William S. Campbell, Kathy Ehrensperger, Philip Esler, Petri Luomanen, Aaron Kuecker, Mark Nanos, Scott Bartchy, Robert Brawley, David Rudolph, Justin Hardin, Joel Willitts, Chris Zoccali, Ryan Heinsch, Zach Johnson, and Dan Thorpe. Their influence is seen throughout. I want to thank my family for their help in making the sabbatical successful. Amber, Ashley, Alexandria and John Bodkin, Annaliese, and Abigail all contributed to making the sabbatical memorable and refreshing. I am most grateful for your constant love and support as I seek to balance family and vocation. Finally, to my parents, Joseph and Ann Tucker, you continue to be amazing examples of love and faithfulness.

> J. Brian Tucker
> Moody Theological Seminary

1

INTRODUCTION

INTRODUCTION

WHAT TYPE OF BOOK do you have in your hands? It is not a traditional scriptural overview, though the key introductory issues, social background, and central contents of 1 Corinthians are covered. Instead, this volume explores the way 1 Corinthians constructs social identity. It comments on those aspects of the letter that seem to have a decisive impact on the social identity shaping processes of the original audience. It sheds light on these processes through the lens of Henri Tajfel's and John Turner's social identity and self-categorization theories. The combination of these two theories has become the dominant way for social psychologists to study group processes in the United Kingdom and Australia. Within biblical studies they have emerged as the principal social-scientific lens for studying the biblical text, producing a steady flow of dissertations, books, and articles.

READING 1 CORINTHIANS

BRIEF OVERVIEW OF TAJFEL AND TURNER

To begin, a snapshot of Tajfel's and Turner's work as it relates to this work is appropriate.[1] Tajfel and Turner suggest that people gain their identity not only from their self-conception but also from the groups to which they belong. This is, first, because groups provide a positive social identity which facilitates self-respect. Second, individuals seek to avoid anxiety over their behavior. Belonging to groups provides a set of norms according to which one can model one's own behavior and assess the behavior of others.

Members of groups categorize themselves according to the norms and expectations of the group. To the extent that members conform to the norms of the group, they are accepted within it. However, acting against expected norms is viewed as deviancy by fellow group members and can lead to marginalization and rejection. Thus, there are strong social pressures to adopt the norms of the group to which members belong (the ingroup) since this guarantees acceptance. Group norms tend to accentuate similarities between members and minimize differences. Thus an ideal prototype of the group emerges, one who embodies the similarities that group members share, and that also distinguish them from members of other groups. Ingroup members have a vested interest in portraying their ingroup in the best possible light since this reinforces their own sense of worth. Consequently, as ingroup members prefer the norms of their own ingroup in comparison with somewhat similar outgroups, ingroup bias develops.

Members of the ingroup not only categorize themselves according to the norms of the ingroup but also in contrast to the characteristics of outgroups (as the ingroup sees them). To strengthen the positive identity of the

---

1. Esler, "An Outline of Social Identity Theory," 13–39.

Introduction

ingroup, the norms and characteristics of outgroups can be criticized, particularly when the ingroup feels threatened by the outgroup. Such criticism leads to unfavorable stereotyping of outgroup members which, then, leads to prejudice. Negative characteristics are attributed to outgroup members to enhance the feelings of superiority of these members of the ingroup.

FIRST CENTURY MEDITERRANEAN WORLD AND PAUL'S RHETORIC

It might seem odd, at first, to use a contemporary social theory to analyze ancient societies. Are social identity and self-categorization theories applicable to the first century Mediterranean world? Hinkle and Brown have proposed two criteria for the application of social identity and self-categorization models.[2] They argue that, for appropriate use of these models, group identity must be salient for members, in other words, ready to be acted upon. Furthermore, ingroups and outgroups must exist in an atmosphere of competition. Malina, studying the ancient Mediterranean world from an anthropological perspective, claims that both these criteria apply to the ancient Mediterranean world: group identity was more important than personal identity and the pivotal values of the Mediterranean area were honor and shame. Such values, along with patronage, naturally led to an atmosphere of competition between opposing groups in a time when resources were limited.[3]

Jews living in the land of Israel had access to the temple for sacrifice and worship. They, therefore, looked down on Diaspora Jews (those living elsewhere in the Mediterranean

2. Hinkle and Brown, "Intergroup comparisons and social identity," 48–70.

3. Malina, *World*, 45, 58–67, 97–105, 147–48.

world) who were unable to participate in temple rituals. Additionally, their belief in monotheism prohibited Diaspora Jews from being involved in the pagan worship that was often part of civic ceremonies, thus excluding them from much of civic life. Even outside the temple, sacrifices to the gods were part of all-important family celebrations such as marriages or birthdays. Food, particularly meat, wine and oil, which were used in temple sacrifices, were later sold in the market place. Furthermore, marriage laws kept Jews apart from the rest of the civic community since Torah limited intimate relations with gentiles (Gen 34:14; Deut 7:3–4). All these factors resulted in the Jews being isolated and often shunned by gentiles. Yet the very isolation and marginalization of the Jews became an important index of their identity and would affect the identity of the gentiles in Christ who were part of the Christ-movement that was still functioning within the broader synagogue community.

To better understand the nature of Paul's mission-focused discussion, it is important to reflect on these ways that groups are formed and impact identity, since Paul was in fact forming new groups and giving them direction on how to re-orient their lives under their new realization of who they were in Christ. However, this new identity was only one among a number of others that existed, nested one inside the other among the population of Roman Corinth in the mid-first century CE.

Since the early eighties, social psychologists have noted that individual identity does not remain static throughout one's life.[4] Individuals are constantly shifting their self-understanding as they write and speak with others both inside and outside the groups within which they most belong. Groups communicate their definitions of their

4. Tajfel, *Human Groups*, 246; Turner, "The Experimental," 66–101.

ideal member, and individuals align themselves in agreement with or opposition to those definitions. Paul used rhetoric, persuasive language, to address the Corinthian Christ-followers' identity. Corinthian civic identity was in transition in the first century, and that unsettledness, if left uncontested, would ultimately hinder Paul's gentile mission in that important city.

In 1 Corinthians, Paul was intentionally seeking to shape the identity of new Christ-followers, developing the language and practices that he felt necessary for prioritizing their in Christ social identity in a way that supported his gentile mission. Paul's strategy was to transform their Roman identity by forming an alternative community with a distinct set of beliefs and practices, their ethos. To do this, however, he would have to mediate between at least two differing visions of social identity: the imperial ideology of Rome, ultimately, but first the specific concerns of the Christ-following group.

It is important to remember that the Roman empire is never far from Paul's rhetorical strategy. He is forming an alternative community, both in continuity and discontinuity with the broader community, and he seeks to establish an ethos that allows for social integration while maintaining proper boundaries necessary for group identity to develop. The rhetorical situation then is this: Paul is addressing the debates over the social implications of the gospel especially in light of the way existing social identities (ethnic, gender, or socio-economic) are to continue, discontinue, or be transformed in Christ (7:17; 12:13; see also Gal 3:28).

RECENT WORKS ON 1 CORINTHIANS AND SOCIAL IDENTITY

Scholars who have researched 1 Corinthians have recognized that it contains significant material regarding the social setting of the early Christ-movement and is thus particularly suited to social-scientific analysis. The findings of some of these very recent works have shaped my own reading that follows, and may be of interest to readers interested in the ongoing scholarly work on social identity in this letter. Jack Barentsen's *Emerging Leadership in the Pauline Mission* proposes that Paul's model of leadership was similar to that described in Haslam, Reicher, and Platow's *The New Psychology of Leadership*. They argue that for leaders to succeed, they must themselves be examples of the identity that they construct, defend, and embed within their followers. About 1 Corinthians, Barentsen notes the way Paul, as an example of a Jewish follower of Christ, both does and does not fit as a role model for Corinthian gentile believers. Further, he highlights the way the existing leaders in Corinth had been mismanaging the group's identity. Paul, perhaps surprisingly, relies on processes that are found in Tajfel and Turner as he empowers the Corinthians "to strong identity performance."[5] First Corinthians 1–4 along with several other chapters in Corinthians were given a sustained social identity reading in my own books, *You Belong to Christ* and *Remain in Your Calling*, and the findings of these works are condensed throughout this book. Paul's teaching on sexual ethics in 1 Corinthians 5–7 is interpreted using social identity theory in Alistair May's *The Body for the Lord*. He helps readers understand the complexities of group belonging and the psychological nature of group-based problems as they relate to the way the Corinthians

5. Barentsen, *Emerging Leadership*, 100.

were to embody their new identity. First Corinthians 5:1 to 11:1 is given a social identity reading in Sin-Pan Daniel Ho's *Paul and the Creation of a Counter-Cultural Community*. He helps readers to understand the way Paul wants to change the Corinthians' current social practices and values (for example, sexual practices and idolatry) so that these will align more precisely with their new in Christ social identity. Daniel Ho also recognizes that Paul uses Israel's Scriptures and then builds up a new and alternative value system using discussions of Christ. First Corinthians 12–15 is covered from the perspective of social identity and honor-shame by Mark Finney in one of his chapters in *Honour and Conflict in the Ancient World*. Finney makes a particularly strong case for the way worship and belief problems were also identity and honor problems. Finally, 1 Cor 16:1–4 is addressed in my article, "The Jerusalem Collection," which applies the findings of social identity theory to the economic practices Paul discusses there. This present book, building on and expanding all of these insights, offers a sustained reading of the entire letter through the lens of social identity.

PAUL WITHIN JUDAISM IN 1 CORINTHIANS

This book is also written from a post-supersessionist perspective; in other words, it reads Paul as one who does not think that God's covenant with the Jewish people has been made obsolete or that the church has replaced Israel as God's people. This perspective will especially show in those places in the letter where Paul addresses the continued salience of Jewish and non-Jewish identities (1:22–24; 5:8; 7:17–24; 9:19–23; 10:1, 18, 32; 12:13; 16:8). Furthermore, I take Paul's audience to be the gentile Christ-followers in Corinth (12:2). That does not mean that there were not Jews among the congregation; there were. However, Paul's primary focus is on the formation of gentile identity in Christ, helping them to see how this group relates to the God of Israel, the people of Israel, and the broader synagogue community of which the movement is still a part. This approach is essentially different from a more traditional reading, in that I take Paul to be urging distance not from Judaism but rather from the Roman empire.

Such a post-supersessionist approach, like the social identity reading discussed above, also relies on previous works that should be briefly highlighted. William S. Campbell's *Paul and the Creation of Christian Identity* argues for a particularistic understanding of Christ-movement identity, one in which existing identities are not obliterated (7:17–24). Gentile Christ-followers are not to be confused with Israel nor are they the New Israel, or Israel redefined. Instead, God offers an inclusive salvation to Jews as Jews and gentiles as gentiles. Two of Kathy Ehrensperger's works are crucial to the reading put forth here: *Paul and the Dynamics of Power* and *Paul and the Crossroads of Cultures*. These books further highlight Paul's work as an empowering rather than domineering leader, a bicultural mediator between Greek, Roman, and Jewish identities, and one who reasons with Israel's Scripture within its tradition rather than out of it. Further, Ehrensperger contends that key aspects of Roman social identity are incompatible with the exclusive loyalty required in worshipping the God of Israel. Peter Tomson's work, *Paul and the Jewish Law*, highlights the way Paul's teaching has its basis in halakah, the various streams of traditional applications of Torah, while David Rudolph's reading of 1 Cor 9:19–23 in *A Jew to the Jews* opens up the possibility of Paul's continued Torah observance. Finally, Mark Nanos's influence is evident throughout this work, especially his suggestion that the Christ-movement still exists within the synagogue community, that therefore its identity

Introduction

is formed within its Jewish context, and that pre-existing ethnic identities continued to be relevant.[6]

PREVIEW OF THE REST OF THE BOOK

The reading of 1 Corinthians that follows seeks to clarify the identity processes evident in the text. It presupposes that Paul and the Christ-movement do not yet have a separate institutional identity. It also takes Paul's "rule in all the churches" that existing identities matter as its hermeneutical key (7:17). For gentiles, these identities are part of God's good creation and crucial to the gentile mission. For Jews, Paul's rule supports their continuing covenantal relationship with God but also reminds gentiles that they have not replaced Israel as God's people, and that Jewish identity is not incompatible with Paul's gospel.

This book is designed to serve as a running commentary on the letter with the assumption that readers will have a copy of the Bible open beside them, preferably the New Revised Standard Version (NRSV), which is quoted throughout. The reader may find it useful to have a Study Bible close as well, to gain a quick overview of a passage before or while reading this book. *The Jewish Annotated New Testament* may be particularly useful for this purpose since it shares the Israel-centric perspective of this book and is based on the NRSV. Furthermore, John M. G. Barclay's "1 Corinthians" commentary in *The Oxford Bible Commentary* would allow readers to compare some of the ideas offered here with the standard, though social-scientifically informed, view. Finally, a book like this cannot hope to stress everything needed to explain the letter, so

---

6. Nanos and Zetterholm, *Paul within Judaism*, is the most up-to-date and accessible entry point into Nanos's work specifically and this approach to Paul generally. Nanos, "Paul and Judaism," 117–60.

readers may want to consider Edward Adams and David Horrell's edited volume, *Christianity at Corinth*, for many of the essays that have most influenced 1 Corinthians scholars. For a more in-depth next step, Roy Ciampa and Brian Rosner's *The First Letter to the Corinthians*, in the Pillar Commentary Series, is the most important current commentary and would provide further adventures in Paul's letter after finishing this book.

DISCUSSION QUESTIONS

1. What are your apprehensions concerning reading 1 Corinthians through the lens of contemporary theories like Tajfel and Turner?

2. It was noted that Mediterranean culture was group oriented. How is that relevant as you begin to read 1 Corinthians? The same was noted as regards the culture being honor-oriented. How might that impact your understanding of the text? Is today's culture oriented toward the group, or toward honor?

3. In the overview of recent works in 1 Corinthians, a lot of work seems to have been done on the social dynamics of the text. How might that help you in a contemporary setting of diversity?

4. Post-supersessionist interpreters argue that Paul continued to identify himself as Jewish. What concerns do you have about that claim? How might supersessionism reveal itself in your contemporary context?

5. What potential weaknesses might there be in taking Paul's rule in all the churches that each person should remain in their calling as the hermeneutical key for reading the whole letter? What alternative hermeneutical key would you suggest?

2

READING 1 CORINTHIANS

INTRODUCTION

SITTING IN A SEMINARY class, I listened as my fellow students wrestled with what Paul had to say in 1 Corinthians about spiritual gifts. This led to a simple question: Can a person's understanding of God and their spiritual experience of him be separated from their identity, i.e., that sense of who they think they are? Some felt that if a person's errant ways were going to be corrected, then that is exactly what must be done. I disagreed. Not only is this not possible, but attempting to separate the inseparable may make the conflict worse. Paul does not try to dislodge the Corinthians from their existing identity; rather, he writes to the Christ-followers in Corinth to provide a sense of identity salience, a vision for a transformed life in Christ in the context of God's good creation of culture. Since the time that Paul had left Corinth, another vision for identity had taken hold, so he writes 1 Corinthians to adjust their understanding of an in-Christ identity and reinforce an ethos centered on Christ crucified and his resurrection. Before we turn to the actual letter there are a few background details that need clarification as we seek to read 1 Corinthians for identity formation.

AUTHORSHIP

First Corinthians is one of the undisputed letters of Paul and one of his main letters along with Romans, 2 Corinthians, and Galatians. Pauline authorship of this letter is generally undisputed; however, Paul may not be the sole author of the letter. In 1:1, "our brother Sosthenes" is described as a co-author or co-sender. Little is known about Sosthenes, though Acts 18:17 describes a person by the same name who was a leader of the synagogue in Corinth. While his exact involvement with the letter's production is unclear, he was at least present during the dictation of it, and Paul understood him to be significant enough to highlight him at the beginning of the letter. While the variation of the personal pronouns (cf. 1:4; 1:18–31; 2:6–16) suggests that Paul was the primary author of the letter, the main point here is to recognize that he was not a lone individual but was part of a broader network of fellow-workers (3:9) involved in a Jewish mission to the (pagan) nations (so similarly Timothy in 2 Cor 1:1; Phil 1:1; 1 Thess 1:1; Phlm 1:1; and Titus in 2 Cor 8:23).

DATE AND PROVENANCE

First Corinthians was likely written sometime between 53–54 CE from Ephesus (16:8). While the debates concerning Pauline chronology are not settled, the discovery of the Delphi Inscription with its reference to Gallio's proconsulship of Achaea from July 1, 51 to July 1, 52, along with the reference in Acts 18:12 linking him with Paul serves as one relatively fixed point for dating. The incident in Acts probably occurred during the summer of 51. If one then follows the broad contours of Acts, Paul leaves Corinth after around 18 months (Acts 18:11) and travels throughout the Mediterranean basin eventually landing in Ephesus (Acts 18:1–22) where he remained for over two years (Acts 18:23—20:1). It is during this stay in Ephesus that Paul wrote 1 Corinthians.

OCCASION

Several disputes had arisen within the Christ-movement in Corinth over the social implications of the gospel. Paul had written an earlier letter to the Corinthian Christ-followers, alluded to in 5:9, in which he described the way he thought that boundaries should be established within the community. However, Paul's instructions were misunderstood and 5:10–13 functions in part to remind them of mission-oriented boundaries within the burgeoning movement that will help them expand Paul's mission to the gentiles. Thus, what we refer to as 1 Corinthians is actually at least the second letter written to the Corinthian Christ-followers. Part of the occasion of the letter is to allow Paul to clarify his prior statements.

The second event that occasioned 1 Corinthians was the arrival of information from "Chloe's people" (1:11). The reference to these unnamed individuals points to ongoing communication within the earliest Christ-movement. They may also be the ones who informed Paul about the problems alluded to in 5:9. Since the founding of these various congregations was a communal activity (Acts 18:1–7), the sort of updates received in 1:11 would be expected. Some of their contents may have motivated the writing of

1 Corinthians. Additionally, Stephanus, Fortunatus, and Achaicus (16:17) likely delivered a return letter written by the Corinthian Christ-assembly. Parts of this letter may be reasonably reconstructed by paying attention to the phrase "now concerning" (*peri de*) throughout the letter (7:1, 25; 8:1; 12:1; 16:1, 12). Paul's responses to their questions represent another aspect of the occasion for this letter. First Corinthians is part of an ongoing conversation between Paul, his co-workers, and the Corinthian Christ-followers over the social implications of the gospel.

PURPOSE

The purpose of 1 Corinthians is to provide guidance concerning the way existing identities have been transformed but remain salient in Christ (7:17–24). The letter offers wisdom about the interactions that arose within the congregation that "belongs to Christ" (1:18–31; 3:23), and between them and others, now that the present form of this world is passing away (2:6; 5:10; 10:31—11:1). Paul responds to both the oral and written reports he has received (1:11; 7:1, 25; 8:1), seeking to make the social implications of the gospel more concrete and to make the cross of Christ and the resurrection central to the life of the community. Ultimately, Paul relates the problems in Corinth to a misunderstanding of the gospel, and he addresses this by structuring his letter broadly around issues that, from a contemporary perspective, can be categorized as identity, ethics, and ethos. If the Corinthian Christ-followers can embody the gospel more fully, then his purpose for writing will have been fulfilled (15:1–4). One concrete embodiment of this will be their participation in the Jerusalem collection (16:1–4), an issue Paul returns to in a later letter (2 Cor 8:13–15).

Reading 1 Corinthians

LITERARY STRUCTURE

The literary structure of the letter seems to follow generally from its occasion and purpose. First Corinthians 1:1–9 functions as a traditional letter opening and thanksgiving while 16:13–24 serves as the letter's closing. The body can generally be organized around the oral report received from those of Chloe's household (1:10—6:20) and the written letter and explanation from Stephanus, Fortunatus, and Achaicus (7:1—16:12). However, this division is not absolute since some of these varying types of reports are interspersed throughout the letter (11:18; 15:12) and some key ideas are not introduced with the "now concerning" (*peri de*) formula (11:2–34; 15:1–58). Although other structures have been proposed, it seems that a social-scientific thematic overlay may plausibly suggest the following. First, after the letter opening (1:1–9), Paul addresses issues in the formation of social identity (1:10—4:21) and wants to clarify the thinking of the community about who they are in Christ. Second, he moves to address issues broadly described as ethics (5:1—11:1), in which individual behaviors are impacted in light of the new identity inscribed in the first four chapters. Third, Paul concludes the body of the letter (11:2—16:12) by addressing issues of ethos, that is, the group identity that emerges from the new way of thinking and the new way of acting taught in the prior sections of the letter. Since issues of identity, ethics, and ethos generally intersect one another, strict divisions between these sections of the letter would not be expected. Yet, in each section, one of these three is foregrounded. Finally, Paul concludes the letter in 16:13–24. For him, the Corinthian Christ-followers need to pay attention to their in Christ identity as it produces a new set of ethical norms for them as individuals, and ultimately results in a new group ethos, one that better embodies Paul's vision for his gospel communities.

IDENTITY FORMATION OUTLINE

The following outline builds on the identity, ethics, and ethos framework. It reflects a general consensus about the broad literary structure although it uses social identity theory labels to reflect the idea that in 1 Corinthians Paul was seeking to make salient an in Christ social identity by reprioritizing key indexes of existing Roman social identifications to form an alternative community with a distinct ethos. Besides the letter opening and closing, there are three major subsections to the letter that are then subdivided into thirteen communication units.

I. Letter Opening (1:1–9)
   A. Foundation: God's Call (1:1–3)
   B. Framework: God's Grace (1:4–9)

II. The Formation of an in Christ Social Identity (1:10—4:21)
   A. Problems: Groups, Baptism, and Patronage (1:10–17)
   B. Paul's Social Categorization: Ingroup and Outgroup (1:18–25)
   C. Calling and the Role of Existing Roman Social Identification (1:26–31)
   D. The Social Identity-Forming Proclamation of Paul (2:1–5)
   E. Hindrance: Over-Reliance on the World's Wisdom and Power (2:6–9)
   F. Solutions: The Spirit and the Mind of Christ (2:10–16)

G. Hindrance: Over-Identification with Old Social Identities (3:1–4)
H. Identity-Forming Metaphors: God's Field, God's Building, and God's Temple (3:5–17)
I. The Group Belonging to God (3:18–23)
J. Self-Examination and Social Categorization in the Christ-Movement (4:1–5)
K. Paul's Identity, Suffering, and Mission (4:6–13)
L. Paul's Kinship Formation (4:14–17)
M. Paul's Empowerment of the Community (4:18–21)

III. The Embodiment of New Ethical Practice (5:1—11:1)
A. Problem: Existing Sexual Identity (5:1–13)
B. Problem: Over-Reliance on Roman Legal Identity (6:1–11)
C. Solution: Christ-Like Embodiment (6:12–20)
D. Problem: Marriage and Pre-Christ-Following Relations (7:1–16)
E. Solution: Remain in Your Calling (7:17–24)
F. Problem: Secondary Gender Identities (7:25–40)
G. Problem: Food Offered to Idols and Civic Engagement (8:1–13)
H. Solution: Balance between Gospel-Informed Rights and Responsibilities (9:1–18)
I. Solution: Mission as Social Identification (9:19–23)
J. Solution: Non-Agonistic Self-Discipline (9:24–27)
K. Problem: Idolatry (10:1–13)

- L. Solution: Gentiles in Christ Formed through Israel's Example and Story (10:14–22)
- M. Solution: Mimesis and Embodiment for God's Glory (10:23—11:1)

IV. The Emergence of a Transformed Group Ethos (11:2—16:12)
   - A. The Continuation of Gender Hierarchies (11:2–16)
   - B. The Transformation of Table Fellowship (11:17–34)
   - C. The Transformation of Existing Identities and Spiritual Gifts (12:1–11)
   - D. The Emergence of Unity amid Diversity in the Spirit (12:12–31)
   - E. An Ethos of Love: A Gospel Identity Made Salient (13:1–13)
   - F. Doxological Identity: An Others-Oriented Communal Practice (14:1–12)
   - G. Doxological Identity: Outward-Oriented Mission Practice (14:13–25)
   - H. Doxological Identity: Limits and Restrictions on Communal Practices (14:26–40)
   - I. Gospel Identity: By God's Grace I Am What I Am (15:1–19)
   - J. Apocalyptic Identity Formation: The Transformation of Views of Death (15:20–34)
   - K. Possible Future Social Identities: Life beyond This Life (15:35–58)
   - L. Economic Social Identity: The Cultivation of Generosity (16:1–4)

M. Partnerships in the Earliest Christ-Movement (16:5–12)

V. Letter Closing (16:13–24)
   A. The Vision for a Transformed Roman Social Identity (16:13–18)
   B. Emergence of a Superordinate Social Identity (16:19–20)

THEMES OF IDENTITY, ETHICS, AND ETHOS IN 1 CORINTHIANS

Identity, ethics, and ethos provide an effective set of categories with which to organize the issues found in 1 Corinthians. Paul pays equal attention to all three as the above outline details. Although he could not have had these specific labels in mind, these contemporary terms serve to organize the material found in the text. In 1 Corinthians 1–4, Paul addresses issues of identity while the rest of the letter answers questions related to ethics and the impact proper individual choices have on the life of the community (in other words, on the resultant ethos of the group). These three categories, however, must be properly defined. First, identity, as a term, has almost lost its communicative value because it is used in so many ways by scholars and lay people alike. For the purposes of this book, identity is composed of several factors that, when combined, contribute to one's understanding of oneself, including the group memberships that affect that understanding. Second, ethics refers to the individual choices and behaviors made by members of the Christ-assembly based on their prior self-understanding. Third, ethos refers to the resultant character of a particular group based on members' ethics and patterns of behavior. Since these, too, have been informed by members' self-understanding, the interrelatedness of the three approaches is clear.

Identity

The theme of identity is seen clearly in 1 Corinthians 15:10a: "by the grace of God I am what I am." This "what I am" must involve one's ethnicity and socio-economic status: "For in the one Spirit we were all baptized into one body—Jews or Greeks, slaves or free—and we were all made to drink of one Spirit." While 12:13 thus highlights the inclusive nature of identity in Christ, 10:32 differentiates an in-Christ identity from two ethnic identities that, nevertheless, are represented also within the congregation. While 12:2 points out that at least one aspect of gentile identity, idol worship, is no longer salient in Christ, 7:17–24 establishes Paul's rule in all the Christ assemblies that existing identities are a matter of calling and are not obliterated in Christ. In the example of female gender identity (11:2–16; 14:34–35), Paul suggests that gender continues in Christ. Further, the distinctions based on the secondary gender identities of "widows" and "virgins" in 7:8, 25 suggest these also continue to be salient in Christ. By far the most problematic existing identity Paul mentions in 1 Corinthians relates to Roman masculinity. The majority of Paul's theologizing in this letter seeks to construe, or interpret, a masculine gender identity brought under the lordship of Christ. He describes it in contrast to prevailing notions of Roman masculinity (16:13), for example, rejecting ownership of one's own body (6:19–20a), and projecting a mutuality of belonging in marriage (7:4). Since, additionally, Paul was single (7:8) and thus did not establish a proper Roman household, key indexes of masculinity are open to modification within the Christ-movement. Such issues related to identity in much of his writing make clear that, for Paul, issues of identity precede the development of his theology.

Ethics and Ethos

Ethics and ethos are more easily noticed when reading this letter since most of it addresses problematic behavior: group discrimination, leadership confusion, aberrant sexuality, greed, idolatry, and social exclusion. The one verse that summarizes Paul's theologizing about ethics and ethos is 1 Cor 10:24: "Do not seek your own advantage, but that of the other." Ethical variety is evident in 7:17–24; 8:7–13; and 9:19–23 with a common in-Christ identity serving as that which orders and maintains communal life amid diversity (3:23; 12:12–31).[1] The closest he comes to uniformity is 1:10, "all of you be in agreement and that there be no divisions among you." There are three reasons why this verse does not obliterate differing ethical implications among Christ-followers (especially for Jews and non-Jews in Christ). First, in 7:17 "Paul's rule in all the Christ-assemblies" is that individuals should remain in the calling in which they were called. This requires differing social practices for Jews and gentiles, and for the married and unmarried, for example (1 Cor 5–11). Second, Paul expects a person's conscience to guide their ethical practices (10:25, 27–29); however, behavior must also be chosen with proper consideration for other group members (8:7, 10, 12). Third, about the resulting group ethos, the continuation of diversity is a key implication of Paul's instruction in 12:4–6, 12–31. Paul's body metaphor endorses differing practices.

    Paul sought to form an alternative community with a distinct ethos, and in such a group the shared experience of the Spirit and of Christ is to be higher in the identity

1. Wolter, "Let No One Seek His Own," 200, 216.

hierarchy than any other indexes of Roman social identity. However, unlike in the traditional reading of Paul's ethics, I propose that he does not seek to obliterate many or even most features of the Christ-followers' earlier identity, thinking, or decision-making practices. One is not in Christ based on a certain set of behaviors or cultural traditions; in-Christ identity must always practically be defined within each behavioral and cultural context. In fact, while there are aspects of non-Jewish identity that do not survive being in Christ, e.g., immorality, idolatry, unscriptural thought patterns, and cultural boasting, the same identity changes are not relevant for in-Christ Jews since their symbolic universe has its foundation in Israel's scriptural tradition. Paul's ethical reasoning is not supersessionistic but may be most clearly summarized in 10:31–32, "So, whether you eat or drink, or whatever you do, do everything for the glory of God. Give no offense to Jews or to Greeks or to the Christ-assembly of God."

DISCUSSION QUESTIONS

1. What does thinking about 1 Corinthians as a co-authored letter, with Paul as part of a team, suggest for a traditional understanding of Paul as the sole apostle to the gentiles?

2. If Paul's purpose in 1 Corinthians was to address the way existing identities remain or should be set aside in Christ, what does that mean for the way you view your gender, ethnicity, or socio-economic identity?

3. One of the problems evident in 1 Corinthians was unscriptural thought patterns (2:10–16). How do you recognize these patterns in your life and faith community?

4. Paul's teaching on sexuality and gender is at odds with much of contemporary society. Is there still relevance for his teaching on sexuality and gender? If so, what is it?

5. Most teachers and pastors focus on issues of ethics and ethos in the biblical text but overlook (or are unaware of) identity-based issues. Why is paying attention to identity crucial when reading 1 Corinthians?

3

CORINTH AND ITS ROMAN CIVIC IDENTITY

INTRODUCTION

THE APOSTLE PAUL WRITES in 1:2, "To the assembly of God that is in Corinth." This strategic colony was near a small land bridge that ran between the Aegean and Ionian Sea, connecting the Peloponnese with the mainland of Greece. Thus, it served throughout its history as a crucial cultural crossroad. However, beginning readers of 1 Corinthians can sometimes conflate the city as it was in ancient Greece with the Roman colony that had replaced it by the time of Paul. For example, some interpreters will highlight the pervasive sexual immorality of Corinth by suggesting that the Greek word "corinthianize," which can mean "practice sexual immorality," indicates the immoral nature of the colony. However, the word was first used by Aristophanes (446–386 BCE), and its connection to Corinth, if it has one,

Corinth and Its Roman Civic Identity

must be located in the distant Greek past. Other writers will point out that there were massive numbers of temple prostitutes at the top of the Acrocorinth in the temple dedicated to Aphrodite. This conclusion comes from a misreading of Strabo and his use of the term "temple prostitutes," which is better understood as "manumitted slave prostitutes." In any case, Strabo was describing the earlier era of Corinth's existence. Furthermore, both Aristophanes and Strabo were using strong rhetorical language to emphasize their points, and one should be careful not to draw historical conclusions for reading 1 Corinthians based on these texts, especially since they are not referring to the Roman colony of the first century.[1] This colony had its own challenges, but they related to civic identity and the various economic and social pressures that developed from trying to function as an outpost of Roman identity in Greece. This chapter then will introduce the reader to the organizational structure of a first-century Roman colony and the concept of civic identity that will undergird a better first-century historical understanding of the colony. It will also show that Corinthian identity was in flux during this time, and that this accounts for some of the social dynamics evident in 1 Corinthians. This chapter will go on to briefly highlight the reasons for the internal conflicts within the community and will address its relations with the civic authorities. Thus, the reader will gain a more historically concrete context for understanding Paul's argument in this letter. Paul writes to address the way an over-identification with key aspects of Roman social identity were causing problems within the local assembly of Christ-followers.

---

1. See further Harrill, *The Manumission of Slaves in Early Christianity*, 70–71; Aristophanes, *Frogs*, 354; Strabo, *Geography*, 8.6.20; 12.3.36; Pausanias, *Description of Greece*, 2.5.1.

READING 1 CORINTHIANS

ROMAN COLONY NOT GREEK CITY

Corinth had flourished as a Greek city from the 8th to the 5th centuries BCE, but its uprising against the Romans led to its destruction in 146 BCE. All that remains of the Greek city are sections of the marketplace, pillars of a central temple, and a fountain. Cicero describes some of this:

> Many Carthaginians were slaves at Rome, many Macedonians after the capture of King Perses. I have seen too in the Peloponnese in my youthful days some natives of Corinth who were slaves. All of them could have made the same lament as that in the *Andromacha*: "All this did I see . . . ," but by the time I saw them they had ceased, it may be, to chant dirges. Their features, speech, all the rest of their movements and postures would have led one to say they were freemen of Argos or Sicyon; and at Corinth the sudden sight of the ruins had more effect upon me than upon the actual inhabitants, for long contemplation had had the hardening effect of length of time upon their souls (Cicero, *Tusculan Disputations*, 3.22).

Julius Caesar rebuilt Corinth in 44 BCE as a Roman colony and named it "The Colony Corinth, to the Praise of Julius." Strabo recounts some of this:

> Now after Corinth had remained deserted for a long time, it was restored again, because of its favorable position, by the deified Caesar, who colonized it with people that belonged for the most part to the freedmen class (Strabo, *Geography*, 8.6.23).

The majority of the population was Greek, but a large number of Roman military veterans, according to Plutarch,

Corinth and Its Roman Civic Identity

lived there as well, with a sprinkling, according to Appian, of the urban poor from Rome, Phoenicians, and Phrygians.

> And in the effort to surround himself with men's good will as the fairest and at the same time the securest protection, he again courted the people with banquets and distributions of grain, and his soldiers with newly planted colonies, the most conspicuous of which were Carthage and Corinth (Plutarch, *Life of Caesar*, 57.8).

In the New Testament, the Roman character of Corinth is reflected in the many Latin names associated with it: Aquila, Priscilla, Crispus, Lucius, Gaius, Tertius, Erastus, Quartus, Fortunatus, and Achaicus.[2] The Latin nature of these names is not often mentioned by interpreters, but they match the accounts of the ancient authors.

Corinth became the capital of the Roman province of Achaea in 27 BCE. Old temples were restored and enlarged, new shops and markets were built, new water supplies were developed and old ones restored, and many public buildings were added. This new construction all had distinctively Roman architectural elements. By the first century, Corinth's marketplace, or public center, was larger than any in Rome, and in 50 CE, when Paul visited Corinth, it was the most beautiful, modern, and industrious city of its size in Greece.

Colonies in the Roman world had charters that established their relationship to Rome. The civic charter for Corinth has disappeared; however, one can discern the contours of its structure from a comparative analysis of the charter for Urso, Spain, as well as from the inscriptions and coins in Corinth (Urso, Spain; *Inscriptiones Latinae Selectae*, 6087). The population of Corinth was made up of

2. Hunt, *The Not-Very-Persecuted Church*, 38–39.

both citizens and residents; they had various levels of voting privileges, but only the citizens were entitled to hold office. Those who could vote were divided into tribal assemblies whose legislative functions were limited to annually electing the two magistrates of the colony and the two commissioners for public works.[3]

The local senate, chosen from among ex-magistrates, had significant political powers and oversaw the day-to-day operations (water usage, roads, buildings, and security) of the colony. Local senators were required to own land or to have previously been elected as a magistrate or a public works commissioner. Another group of magistrates was elected every fifth year; they were charged with taking a census of the population. The local senate contained one hundred members, and, if there were not enough ex-magistrates available, eminent individuals could be chosen for these positions.

The two magistrates presided over civil cases in the colony as well as the meetings of the local senate and administrators. Their primary role was to implement legislation passed by the administrators. The qualifications for a magistrate were similar to those of the administrators; furthermore, by the time of Augustus, in the late 1st century BCE, the position was limited to free born citizens. The names of the administrators, for example Gnaeus Publius and Marcus Antonius Orestes, who had also been magistrates for the census in 40 BCE, can be found on coins minted in Corinth. Gnaeus Babbius Philinus also served in a number of these and other offices and is known from a monument erected in his honor.

The two commissioners for city works served as the colony managers, running the marketplace, presiding over

---

3. Engels, *Roman Corinth*, 16–18. This section draws significantly on his work.

commercial disputes, and organizing the local Isthmian games, an event on the order of the Olympics, held in the honor of Poseidon, and celebrated every two years in Corinth. They had lost their power to command since the end of the Republic (27 BCE). The commissioners for city works were not in positions of power equivalent to the magistrates, and their influence was felt primarily in their responsibilities for the revenue of the colony. The name of a commissioner for city works, Erastus, can be seen on an inscription dated to the mid-first century CE in Corinth.

The president of the sacred games was elected biennially. He would have been expected to fund the games himself, so he would have been among the wealthiest of the Corinthian citizens. He had a board of ten Greek judges who provided logistical support for the pan-Hellenic games, which included the Olympic, Pythian, Nemean, along with the Isthmian. These games combined to support the construction of a trans-local Greek identity that drew on their shared mythology, e.g., that found in Homer's *Iliad* and *Odyssey*.

CIVIC IDENTITY IN TRANSITION

The Roman sacred cults were experiencing transition and redefinition during this period. The senate, however, still made the final decisions concerning these transformations. The developing civic identity included one's allegiance to a systematic set of moral and political beliefs, a personal ideology of sorts, to which residents were expected to commit themselves. The emotional and moral components of these beliefs were a devotion to one's community and a sense of responsibility to the society at large. The maintenance of civic identity within the empire was enforced by Roman officials and the provincial collaborators if too much religious liberty was exercised. For example, they suppressed the Bacchic cult in 186 BCE.

The Romans, like other sovereign city-states in the ancient Mediterranean, saw clear connections between religious identity and socio-political authority. As they acquired an empire, the Romans supported and maintained this civic religion among their subjects. Colonies like Corinth were allowed to retain and control their own sacred cults. However, the civic model of religion would soon prove inadequate, and this instability provided a void for the missional work of Paul and his collaborators.[4] Furthermore, because the earliest Christ-movement emerged within the instability of Corinthian civic identity in the mid-first century, it did not experience significant external pressure from provincial collaborators.

This situation is reflected in the two Corinthian letters that have survived which provide evidence for significant contact, but little conflict, with outsiders. First Corinthians specifically shows that the relationship with those outside the believing community provided effective opportunities for extending the Pauline mission; however, this relationship also created a number of the problems within the assembly. Paul ultimately presents this relationship as helpful but provides, in 1 Corinthians, guidelines for how these relationships should proceed. Paul's writing should be seen as a continuation of his missional vocation which included initial evangelism, community formation, and ongoing nurture (3:1–2; 4:15).

In 4:8–13 Paul describes the Corinthians' experience as lacking many of the difficulties that Paul himself had experienced. In Corinth, as in other locations in the Roman east, a person's wealth and status were highly valued. However, the demographic makeup of the colony, including

4. Finney, *Honour and Conflict*, 60–63.

Corinth and Its Roman Civic Identity

the freedmen and retired military may have heightened this emphasis (4:8; 2 Cor 8:14).[5] The Corinthian assembly was made up of individuals of wealth and status who would have been impacted by a significant number of the boundaries inherent in Paul's preaching, boundaries which they may have misunderstood or simply chosen not to follow.

In 6:1–11, Paul argues that the Corinthian Christ-followers may be putting too much confidence in the court system. The courts were not accessible to the majority of individuals in the Roman empire, so the fact that Corinthian Christ-followers were engaged in litigation argues for people of some means, who at least owned land. Paul critiques the Christ-followers for allowing those on the outside of the movement to judge their disputes. Instead, their confidence should be in the believing community and their ability to rule on problems, or, better, they should be willing to be wronged because of their new identity in Christ (6:7).

The Corinthians' good social relations with outsiders may also be seen in their willingness to participate in the cultic meals in the various temples in Corinth (8:7–13). Since religion, in Corinth, was not separate from civic identity, many of the Corinthians did not see a problem with continuing this practice. The wide variety in the economic and social status of the believers in Corinth may have reinforced this practice since the small group of elites might think attendance at these functions could support the gentile mission (a problem that would not be a concern for slaves who would not have the same opportunity). Paul, however, understands that this practice had broader implications for his mission, so he prioritizes conscience and brotherly love in his instructions.

---

5. Millis, "The Local Magistrates and Elite of Roman Corinth," 38–53.

As an extension of the previous arrangements, Corinthian Christ-followers also dined with outsiders in their homes and in other communal settings (1 Cor 10:27—11:1). If the Christ-followers in Corinth were not involved in the civic life of the community, one would not expect this to be a significant issue for them. They appeared to not sense the need to change their approach to their civic life once they had accepted Paul's gospel. Paul ultimately argues they may continue these eating practices; however, their social ethics should seek the benefit of others and not just focus on themselves.

Paul also notes that outsiders were visiting the houses that were being used for worship (14:1–25), which shows that their worship gatherings were open to those who did not believe in Paul's gospel. Who would these outsiders include? They could be unbelievers, spouses, or guests; in any case, Paul addresses the vanity of the Christ-followers and suggests that they present themselves in an orderly way, so that the outsiders might not think they are "mad."

Paul presents the relationships that the Corinthian Christ-followers have with outsiders, on the whole, as good, and he provides guidance on how to interact with them. Paul sees an opportunity for mission in their civic connections and encourages behaviors that will further his mission in Corinth. How did the Corinthians come to possess this type of relationship with outsiders? The transitional nature of Corinthian civic identity may be seen as the primary reason for the openness of civic leaders to these followers of Jesus and can be contrasted especially with Thessalonica where such openness did not exist (Acts 17:1–9; 2 Thess 2:14–16).

INTERNAL CONFLICTS IN THE CORINTHIAN CHRIST-MOVEMENT

Wealth was the vital indicator of status in the pre-industrial, agrarian society of the Roman empire. The general consensus has been that the Christ-followers in Corinth came from a cross-section of rich and poor, categories that reveal the unmeasurable grid of social status. Thus, scholars have sought to develop models of poverty or economy that make the economic profile of the congregation more explicit. The results suggest that the vast majority of the group was at, or right above, the subsistence level and that none of the individuals mentioned by name were from the imperial elite. However, there may have been some individuals with a measure of surplus wealth: Chloe (1:11), Phoebe (Rom 16:1–2), and Erastus (Rom 16:23). Thus, the Pauline community at Corinth closely mirrored the economic structure within the broader civic community.

First, the majority of the Pauline community was poor, as was Paul (2 Cor 11:1–21). It is interesting to note that these people are never mentioned as individuals, only as a group. This is a further indicator of their economic status (cf. 16:1–2; 2 Cor 8:12–15). Among this group are "small farm families, laborers (skilled and unskilled), artisans (especially those employed by others), wage earners, most merchants and traders, [and] small shop/tavern owners."[6] Some within the community would have been wealthier than Paul, which was likely to present him with some difficulty as he attempted to lead them.

There were, furthermore, a few individuals of a higher economic status. Chloe appears to be a woman of moderate surplus resources, at the same level as a merchant, a trader, a freed-person, an artisan who employ others, or a military

6. Friesen, "Demography," 365.

veteran. There is not enough evidence for an evaluation of Phoebe; she appears to be a helper/leader in Cenchraea, but, if she had been a member of the elite, she would not have needed a letter of recommendation from Paul (Rom 16:1–2). It is safe, however, to at least place her on the same level as Chloe. Erastus, too, may be a part of the ruling elite since, in Rom 16:23, he is described as the "city treasurer." He was probably not a part of the municipal elites, yet he would still be someone with moderate surplus resources.[7]

One last group should be mentioned. In 11:22, some appear to be lacking food during the Lord's Supper, so apparently individuals from a lower economic class than the majority of the members of the community were among them. They lived below the level of subsistence and can be described as "farm families, unattached widows, orphans, beggars, disabled persons, unskilled day laborers, [and] prisoners."[8] This group and the implications of their identity will be discussed in the next section.

RELATIONS WITH CIVIC AUTHORITIES

There was little interaction between the ruling elites and those living at the poverty level, and this rigid hierarchy of status was reinforced by law. The divisions were, for example, between freeborn and slaves (7:21–22; 12:23), citizen (limited to adult males) and non-citizen; in each case, the former had the ability to take someone from the latter group to court (6:1–11). Among the citizens, there were various orders or ranks that were grounded in the Roman families to which they belonged. The Roman senatorial class was the most elite and wealthy while the Roman equestrians were similar to the senators economically but beneath

7. Goodrich, *Paul as an Administrator*, 12, 62–63.
8. Friesen, "Demography," 365.

them in status. In colonies like Corinth, the elites would have been the local senators; each of these classes had significant property qualifications for membership, while the rest classified as plebs. Among the freeborn, privileged and non-privileged were defined by law and had certain rights within the judicial system. Those taking others to court in 6:1–11 may have been from this freeborn class.

Public appearance was central to establishing and maintaining status. Roman senators wore a broad purple striped toga, while the purple stripe on the toga of equestrians was narrow. There were numerous laws passed to protect the symbols that were worn in public and communicated status.

Relationships between those of differing status were further regulated by traditions which expressed notions of respect and deference. Patronage, for example, a hierarchical relationship in which parties exchange honor and favors, functioned to inscribe status differences, although not everyone was involved in a patron-client relationship. However, some of the issues Paul addressed seem to be related to individuals resisting this hierarchical structure (e.g., 1 Corinthians 5–7). They may, in fact, have seen this resistance in Paul, himself, who does not accept their possible offers to become a client (9:1–18).

This social system, despite its sharp class divisions, provided much needed social cohesion. The Pauline community appears to have been mostly populated by individuals living at the subsistence level, while a small group may have had moderate to surplus financial resources (1:26). They struggled for prestige and influence, imitating what they had done within the broader community of Corinth. Even among the dependents of a single person of prestige, there was likely to be competition for positions closer to the person in the center. This may have produced factions

(1:12) as those nearest the person of influence became more influential themselves, and collected their own circle of influence.

CONCLUSION

The Roman social context thus seems to have created a significant number of the problems that Paul addresses in this letter. Corinth's civic identity was in flux during this period. Thus, the Corinthians' openness to a new religious movement was quite different from the response to Paul's gospel in other parts of the empire. The situation therefore allowed for more interaction with those who had not yet become convinced of the gospel message, but it also established a climate in which too many Roman imperial social practices could develop within the movement itself. Paul does not seek to remove this influence; he tempers it. He is convinced that existing identities are missionally significant, and thus what is needed in Corinth is a reprioritization of key aspects of Roman social and civic identity rather than a complete obliteration of them (if that were even possible). This is a rather nuanced argument, and it is no wonder that the Corinthians may have initially misunderstood Paul's teaching. There was a need to clarify the social implications of the gospel at this crucial cultural crossroads (5:9–11).

DISCUSSION QUESTIONS

1. How does understanding Corinth as a Roman colony rather than as a Greek city help in understanding the economic, cultural, and social problems in the letter? Why do you think there is such a fascination today with ideas of pervasive sexual immorality among the Corinthians? Is there an over-emphasis on sexual

Corinth and Its Roman Civic Identity

immorality among some church groups?

2. Do you think that there is a temptation to identify too closely with civic and governmental identities today? What causes followers of Christ to rely too much on political power and prestige? What, if any, is the appropriate role of civic identity within the church?

3. This chapter introduced the idea of mission as social identification. What would it mean to identify closely with the broader culture for missional purposes? Are you personally tempted to accommodate or to escape from the broader culture?

4. Part of the problem in Corinth related to the differing social groupings that existed in the wider city. In what ways do you see social class disparity as a cause for problems within the church today? Why do you think that Christ-followers often gravitate towards those close to their social status? How can social alienation within the church be overcome?

5. Ancient Roman society was structured around patronage. Do you think Paul wanted to completely reverse this structure or transform it (in other words, redeploy it for gospel purposes)? What are the societal ordering principles active today, and what would it mean to see these transformed? Are Christ-followers responsible to seek peace, justice, and equity in the broader society or only within the church?

4

"BE UNITED IN THE SAME MIND AND THE SAME PURPOSE" (1:1—2:16)

INTRODUCTION

BECAUSE OF THE HISTORY of race relations in America, racial reconciliation discussions generally polarize groups that otherwise have a lot in common. There are two broad approaches to existing racial identities within the church. Some believe that in Christ existing identities have been erased and what really matters is our shared identity in Christ. However, "our shared identity in Christ" usually turns out looking quite similar to white culture, so this position can mask a political power move behind theological language. Another approach argues that in-Christ believers are one, but existing differences are not erased and, in fact, should be celebrated as part of God's good creation. In this second view, identities should transform in some ways as they are brought under the lordship of Christ, but to call for their obliteration is a mistake. This issue of racial reconciliation in the church confronts the nature of unity amid diversity.

Paul's circumstances were different, but when he argues that the Corinthians should have the same mind and purpose, he is not arguing for uniformity that erases existing identities. He is in line with the second approach mentioned above, one that sees racial and ethnic identities as crucial to the formation of an in-Christ identity. The first part of the opening section of this letter lays the foundation and framework for Paul's particularistic approach to identity. He then discusses problems of existing identities, group categorizations, calling in Christ, and the gospel message. He confronts the major hindrance to identity salience in Corinth and offers his solution. Throughout, Paul addresses issues of identity, after which he will turn his attention to specific ethical issues that give rise to a group ethos. For Paul, all three of these should work together: identity, ethics, and ethos.

FOUNDATION: GOD'S CALL (1:1-3)

First Corinthians 1:1–9 functions as a traditional letter opening and thanksgiving, yet not so much so that Paul, as an entrepreneur of identity, is unable to address the core identity issue: the need to reestablish the Corinthians' in Christ identity. Paul lays this foundation in 1:1 by referring to himself as an apostle, positioning him to influence social identity as a divinely called leader. Calling discourse is central to much of Paul's identity-forming work in this letter (1:1, 2; 7:17–24). However, Paul is not doing this work alone; he will highlight others he calls co-workers (4:17) and Sosthenes is mentioned as one of these (cf. Acts 18:17). God's call is through Christ to be in Christ, and that call will have differing social implications for various subgroups throughout this letter (7:18; 11:4–5).

Social identity is that part of a person's self-concept derived from their membership in a group along with the value they associate with that membership. Paul, in 1:2–3, calls his addressees "the church (*ekklēsiai*) of God in Corinth." This is a group label connected to Paul's Jewish tradition (Exod 12:6), and at this early stage it specifically described the Pauline Christ-movement. Although it eventually developed into the generic group term "church," the NRSV's translation of *ekklēsia* as "church" in Paul's letter is anachronistic and may suggest an institutional setting from a later period after the clear separation from Judaism. The Greek term *ekklēsia* might be better translated as "congregation," "assembly," "Christ-assembly," or "Christ-group."

Paul continues to form the Corinthians' identity by naming them "those who are sanctified in Christ Jesus, called to be saints." This indexes their identity by means of holiness discourse and expresses his sense of who they are (even in light of some of their deviant behavior discussed later in the letter; 6:18). Paul continues to redraw the boundaries around the community by connecting them with "all those who in every place call on the name of our Lord Jesus Christ." For Paul, an in-Christ identity goes beyond local congregations; there is a superordinate identity that is shared among those in Christ. This shared lordship will be crucial for the way Paul reprioritizes existing identities (6:13). He closes the salutation by highlighting "grace" and "peace," ideas that will be important for Paul's rhetorical vision for the Corinthians' communal ethos. Paul then grounds his thankfulness in God's grace which, as he will explain in the next several verses, functions as his identity framework.

FRAMEWORK: GOD'S GRACE (1:4-9)

For Paul, in 1:4-9, the foundation of identity is God's calling in Christ, which explains his emphasis on staying when called (7:20). But the framework of identity is God's grace, understood as the process of responding to God's gift.[1] These processes relate to the Corinthians' speech, knowledge, and testimony. The "grace of God" results in them being "enriched in speech and knowledge." These two components are central to Greek and Roman social identity. They likely serve as places of contact between the Christ-followers and their existing cultural identity. Speech and knowledge should not become skills to boast about. These gifts "strengthened" their "testimony" and, thus the Corinthian Christ-followers ought to recognize God and not themselves as the source of these gifts. After naming the community and reminding them of their calling, Paul points them toward a possible future social identity.[2] He characterizes them as having an abundance of "spiritual gifts" that build up the group as they "wait for the revealing (*apokalypsis*) of our Lord Jesus Christ." This apocalyptic eschatological perspective suggests that Paul saw a future component to an in-Christ identity; it was those in Christ who would be found "blameless on the day of our Lord Jesus Christ."

Paul concludes his thanksgiving by declaring that "God is faithful" and that the Corinthian Christ-followers have been "called into the fellowship (*koinōnia*) of his Son."

1. Barclay, *Paul and the Gift*, 577-78.
2. Cinnirella, "Exploring Temporal Aspects of Social Identity," 230-33.

This *koinōnia* is a shared communal life together with its source in the work of Christ. The Messiah Jesus serves as an anti-imperial figure against the pretensions of the Roman empire, with its boast to have united all the peoples of the world (2:6–9). The fellowship of the called is the superordinate group with which the Corinthians are to relate most, above their allegiance to the provincial governing authorities or any other expression of Roman imperialism in the Greek east, whose power is fleeting (2:6). The foundation and framework for identity is in Christ which Paul establishes within the communal life of the Corinthian Christ-followers in 1:1-9 through naming, calling, and apocalyptic eschatology.

PROBLEMS: GROUPS, BAPTISM, AND PATRONAGE (1:10–17)

The body of the letter begins, in its first major section, with the formation of an in Christ social identity (1:10—4:21). This section is about belonging. The cognitive, evaluative, and emotional elements of a group are functioning inadequately in Corinth, so Paul writes to restore the salience of the group's in Christ social identity. He starts in 1:10: "I appeal to you, brothers and sisters . . . that all of you be in agreement and that there be no divisions among you." This encourages his fellow siblings to embody a transformed identity in their everyday life (e.g., "same mind" and "same purpose"). The unity that Paul seeks centers on the continuing reality of Jesus Christ within the community, but this unity is not an unswerving uniformity that obliterates difference. His "rule in all the churches" is that diverse callings continue (7:17). His reliance on "conscience" for ordering social life (10:25, 27–29), though tempered by its orientation to others, supports the continuation of difference (8:7,

"Be United in the Same Mind and the Same Purpose" (1:1—2:16)

10, 12). Finally, a key social implication of Paul's body metaphor (12:4–6, 12–31) is diversity amid unity. The use of "mind" and "purpose" point to the cognitive and emotional components of social identity formation. In 2:16, the "mind" becomes a metaphor for the integration of the community, while in 14:14–15, 19 it is the mark of an effective community. Paul combines the evaluative and emotional elements of "purpose" when he addresses some of the matters that have caused division (7:25, 40; 2 Cor 8:10), issues where Paul allows for differences.

Paul affirms the Corinthians as part of his kinship group; they are his "brothers and sisters" (1:11). He tells them that he has received a report that there are "quarrels" within the group which have led to the "divisions" mentioned in 1:10. His focus on behavior in this passage is evident when one realizes that negotiation and self-presentation are key processes highlighted by social identity theory when addressing internal conflicts.[3] Such intra-group interaction is evident in 1:11, but the actual cause for the divisions are detailed in 1:12. The entire community has divided over which prototypical figure they are to follow, to belong to, and with whom to primarily identify: "Paul," "Apollos," or "Cephas." "Christ" was added by Paul for rhetorical effect since a separate group claiming to follow Christ is not mentioned again. Furthermore, the general argument in this letter is that Paul is encouraging the Corinthians to see themselves as belonging to Christ (3:4, 21–22, 23). Paul's concern, however, is that the Christ-followers in Corinth were identifying with certain sub-groups to enhance their own importance, and this kind of behavior can often threaten existing ingroup identity. Since Paul is now aware that there are "quarrels," he expresses his desire that the Corinthians be of the "same mind and same

3. Hogg and Abrams, *Social Identifications*, 4–5.

purpose" (1:10). Then he shifts his attention to misunderstandings about leadership, baptism, and patronage.

Leaders who had baptized an individual or a household were being treated by some as their patron. In 1:13, Paul writes, "Has Christ been divided?" Each subgroup from 1:12 may have been claiming its own portion of Christ. Perhaps they heard Paul's call for diversity as an implicit suggestion that there was no need for unity. Perhaps they were divided over different ways to understand Christ (1 Cor 12). In any case, dividing Christ was an inappropriate idea for a community that belongs to him (3:23). Paul then asks two rhetorical questions: "Was Paul crucified for you? Or were you baptized in the name of Paul?" The message of the cross should define the community's identity. Baptism, too, is an identity-forming experience. Paul uses them together to show that the community has a fundamental misunderstanding concerning the social implications of the gospel, especially as it relates to the Christ-followers' identification with group leaders or prototypes. In fact, in 1:14–15, Paul is thankful that his involvement with baptisms within the community was minimal because this would have inadvertently contributed to the division within the congregation. He did, however, baptize "Crispus" (Acts 18:8), "Gaius" (Rom 16:23), and "the household of Stephanas" (16:17). These particular baptisands may have contributed to the association of baptism with patronage, especially since these were individuals of some means. Such divisions are not necessarily evidence of theological disagreements; they could simply have arisen from normal processes of social categorization. Baptism, Paul explains, is meant to define social identity in relation to Christ, not in relation to the person who performed the baptism.

The baptisms mentioned in 1:16 include another component of Roman social identity: "the household," in this case Stephanas's. Paul's involvement in their baptisms could explain the way social identity, intragroup behavior, and group belonging become issues. If Stephanas and his household aligned themselves with Paul, and others did not, it suggests that the person who baptized a household then became its group prototype. Paul appears to take advantage of this allegiance in 16:16, where he instructs the Christ-group to be in the "service" of these early baptisands and their co-workers. He does, therefore, expect that some important aspects of Roman social identity, such as kinship and household structures, will continue within the Christ-movement. Those in Stephanas's household, for example, were under his authority. However, there seems to have been disagreement about the nature of the continuation of this social structure. Was it obliterated, transformed, or reprioritized in Christ? The centrality of the household within civic life and the boundary-crossing event of baptism combine to form a contact zone of identity, especially in those situations where women and slaves, who were otherwise marginalized by Roman water practices (such as in public baths), became equal members of the community through this rite (Gal 3:28).

In 1:17, Paul summarizes his argument concerning the Corinthians' lack of understanding of their in-Christ social identity. For Paul, Christ is the "power" and "wisdom" of God (1:24), and therefore the primary identity-forming discourse for the group. He reminds them that he was sent to "proclaim the gospel" not to "baptize." Paul may be distancing himself from his own responsibility for some of the confusion over the social function of baptism. Paul asserts social influence by reminding the Christ-followers that his primary purpose was to proclaim "the gospel." He is not disparaging baptism, but pointing to the way it was defining social identity, as shown by the subgroup social identification in 1:12. Paul argues that anything that obscures "the cross of Christ" within the community must be de-emphasized, and this includes certain aspects of Roman social identity, such as households and bathing practices.

PAUL'S SOCIAL CATEGORIZATION: INGROUP AND OUTGROUP (1:18–25)

In 1:18, Paul categorizes people into two social groups, one positive and the other negative. Those within the outgroup, "those who are perishing," understand the gospel "message" as "foolishness." The ingroup, on the other hand, is called "we who are being saved" (similarly 2 Cor 2:15) and includes those who think the gospel "is the power of God." This is designed to realign the Corinthians' own social categorizations in the hope of adjusting their current levels of intergroup discrimination. They are embracing local aspects of their Roman social identity which need to be somewhat devalued (although not obliterated) in light of the gospel. To further his claim, in 1:19, he cites Isaiah 29:14 to assert that no other system of wisdom ultimately leads to salvation. In 1:20, Paul engages in social stereotyping as he positions three groups outside the ingroup. Social identity is shaped by one's membership in groups, and here Paul makes it clear that not all group memberships are equally beneficial: "Where is the wise? Where is the scribe? Where is the debater of this age?" These three characteristics of groups in the broader Roman society represent, in Paul's discourse, any attempt to secure salvation by means of wisdom. He thereby attempts to resocialize the Corinthians, addressing their general outlook concerning wisdom and salvation, which was still being shaped by this broader community. In 1:21, "God decided to save" them, and they believed that he did so through an event,

"Be United in the Same Mind and the Same Purpose" (1:1—2:16)

the cross, that the world would call foolish. Social identity theory suggests that categorization brings together "social objects" and "system(s) of belief."[4] Paul's categorization here creates an ideological space in which a gospel-shaped social identity may be formed.

Next Paul, in 1:22–24, relies on a social comparison grounded in a particularistic understanding of two ethnic identities, with their two different approaches to wisdom and power. Using stereotypes, Paul notes that "Jews demand signs and Greeks desire wisdom." Similarly, in 1:23, the message of "Christ crucified" is described as a "stumbling block to Jews and foolishness to Gentiles." Paul's argument relies, for its effectiveness, on the comparison of social categories that already existed. He redeploys them for his own broader rhetorical purpose, highlighting the transformation in thinking that had to occur for the Corinthians to accept something they would have previously thought foolish: "Christ crucified." In 1:24, Paul brings up the Corinthians' calling again (1:1–2, 9). He had already established this as the foundation of their identity; now he classifies them ethnically as "both Jews and Greeks." He then points the community back to the centrality of Christ and argues that it is Christ who now is both God's "power" and his "wisdom." These are both key components in the identity-shaping process. Wisdom connects internal belief to external behavior, and power enables this connection to occur. Power, however, may be exercised in either a dominating or an empowering way as identity is formed. Paul empowers the community to transform their identity in Christ and redefines their perception of power: "God's weakness" is understood to be "stronger than human strength" (1:25). The new understanding of social categories and social

---

4. Tajfel, "Social Categorization," 62.

comparisons evident in this passage affects the Corinthians Christ-followers' social identification.

CALLING AND THE ROLE OF EXISTING ROMAN SOCIAL IDENTIFICATION (1:26–31)

Social identification maps similarity and difference through the use of historic references, metaphors, and analogies that combine to ascribe identity. Paul relies on such a process in 1:26 as he focuses on calling and the continuation of existing social identities among the Christ-followers. He highlights a historic reference shared by the community (in other words, a social memory) when he asks them to "consider your own call." Although invisible in English, the "your" here is plural and thus refers to the one call by which all members of the community were brought together in Christ. This past social identification is reinforced by calling them "brothers and sisters." Using kinship language strengthens their identification of each other as part of the same ingroup.

The divisions in Corinth revolved around issues of social identification: barriers had developed among the Christ-followers, who had other social networks with which they could choose to identify. Paul reminds the Corinthians that, when they were called by God to be in Christ, not many of them were considered "wise by human standards," nor "powerful," nor of "noble birth." They were lacking key indicators of Roman social identity "but God chose" them from among those that the elites within the empire would have rejected. This choice by God turns their understanding of "shame" upside down (1:27). God, in fact, puts to shame those who socially identify themselves as wise and powerful. He does this by choosing those who are "despised" and putting an end to those who are wise and powerful (1:28). This means that there are no longer any grounds left for boasting within the community (1:29). In 1:30–31, the implications of following Christ are made obvious as Paul reconstructs the ingroup: Christ is the "wisdom from God." But not only that. He is also "righteousness and holiness and redemption." The identity-forming antithesis introduced in 1:26 is now complete: those who are not wise, powerful, and well-born have become righteous, holy, and redeemed. This describes a gospel-shaped social identity.

THE SOCIAL IDENTITY-FORMING PROCLAMATION OF PAUL (2:1–5)

In 2:1, Paul presents himself as a group prototype who did not rely on the resources of human wisdom when proclaiming the gospel. He reminds the Corinthians that "when" he "came" it was not with "lofty words or wisdom." He negates the influence of Roman identity in relation to speech, whether Greek philosophy (which promoted wisdom) or Roman imperial ideology (which glorified power). Paul's proclamation, his "testimony," following the NRSV marginal reading, was only dependent on "God." He thus again refers to a social memory, that of his own first visit, to construct the community in a way that reaffirms his original rhetorical vision for the straightforward proclamation of the gospel: "Jesus Christ and him crucified" (2:2). Against the twin social pressures of Greek philosophy and Roman imperial ideology, Paul emphasizes Jesus as God's wisdom and power. In 2:3, Paul describes his earlier demeanor as weak and fearful in an effort to reconstruct his preferred ingroup prototype in contrast to those who might rely on philosophical wisdom or political power (Acts 18:9). Paul is convinced that God had already legitimated his message through the work of the "Spirit," and thus he had no need to rely on rhetorical brilliance (2:4). He is specifically seeking to affect the Corinthians' opinions and behaviors related to public teaching. So in 2:5, he wants to be assured that their "faith," which in social identity terms can be defined as their commitment to the norms of behavior within the community, is centered on "the power of God" and not on anything else.

HINDRANCE: OVER-RELIANCE ON THE WORLD'S WISDOM AND POWER (2:6–9)

Paul thinks that the Corinthians' present political system, the Roman empire, is passing away (2:6–9). One way to strengthen ingroup identity is to stereotype the outgroup. Paul thus refers to the Christ-followers in 2:6 as "mature" or wise and contrasts them with the lack of "wisdom" among "the rulers of this age," the ones "doomed to perish." In this way, Paul pushes back against the worldview of the Roman governing authorities that was forming the community ethos. Paul then in 2:7 employs an apocalyptic expression, arguing that "God's wisdom" superseded temporal political empires, such as those of Greek or Rome. Next Paul argues that the Roman empire is not an acceptable option for building a communal ethos because the identity narrative of Roman imperial ideology is flawed. In 2:8, this narrative, that of "the rulers of this age" fundamentally misunderstands God's plan for humankind. The Roman rulers chose to crucify "the Lord of glory" and thus sealed their doom. In 2:9, Paul draws on apocalyptic resources from various places in Israel's Scriptures (Isaiah 64:4; 65:17; Jeremiah 3:16) to encourage a shift in the Corinthians' focus from temporal political power to an apocalyptic eschatology superseding it.

SOLUTIONS: THE SPIRIT AND THE MIND OF CHRIST (2:10–16)

The Spirit is the agent of the wisdom of God within the life of the assembly. Paul includes himself in the ingroup and writes, "these things God has revealed to us through the Spirit." For Paul, God has revealed divine truths, and the communities that form from these truths are then apocalyptic by nature. The Spirit is the one who "searches everything" (2:10) and therefore provides the correct categories for the community's thinking. Social categorization without the guidance of the Spirit produces subgroup divisions such as in 1:11–12, but the presence of the Spirit provides the necessary resources to accurately understand God's wisdom. This, however, includes thinking about one's self, a necessary part of social categorization and the construction of identity (Romans 7:7–25). In 2:12, Paul emphasizes the way those within the community come to know God's wisdom: through the work of the Spirit and not through human wisdom. Of course, it was impossible to escape the standards that the "spirit of the world" imposed; Roman law enforced public compliance. However, Paul was concerned that some were internalizing its norms. This affected the group as its norms shifted to those that did not have their basis in an ethos of faith and love (2:8; 13:2, 13). Paul recognizes, to a certain extent, the need for obeying Rome's laws (Romans 13:1–7), but within the Pauline communities their system causes harm and should not be accepted. Rather, communal existence should be constructed through the work of "the Spirit that is from God." This would allow the community to interpret properly those things that come from the Spirit. "Human wisdom," by contrast, is incapable of properly categorizing reality from God's point of view (2:13). Paul is not arguing against all forms of human wisdom, eloquence, or power. He is only asserting that they are ultimately inconsistent and unreliable resources for the community to use in developing knowledge without the work of the Spirit (2:14–16). Paul labels the outgroup here as the "unspiritual," persons whose identities have not been transformed by the Spirit. Paul contrasts this identity with the "spiritual" (2:15). The "unspiritual" cannot evaluate the "spiritual" because the latter has "the mind of Christ" (2:16). This mindset is the answer to living in unity within the Christ-group in the context of their transformed identities (1:10). This unity does not deny difference (7:20; 8:7–13; 12:12–13) but, as William S. Campbell asserts, neither does it see diversity as a result of human sin, "but as something perfectly in accord with the mind of Christ."[5] The mind of Christ is that which assists the community in living out the social implications of the gospel. It provides the vital decision-making link for negotiating the identity-forming factors of wisdom and power. The Corinthians' identity was in need of construction, primarily because they were too readily identifying with their old social identities, and Paul's argument seeks to guide them in the right direction, toward the Spirit.

DISCUSSION QUESTIONS

1. Paul's goal for the Corinthians is that they be united in mind and purpose. What does this mean in terms of a local faith community? What is the difference between unity and uniformity? How much diversity is acceptable within a congregation before further problems occur? Who decides the course the community will take when there are differences on controversial social issues?

---

5. Campbell, *Paul and the Creation*, 94.

"Be United in the Same Mind and the Same Purpose" (1:1—2:16)

2. The divisions within the group in Corinth related to the leaders or teachers they preferred. Is this still a problem today in churches? What are some practices that might help overcome an over-identification with a leader? Does this have any relevance for the emergence of the celebrity pastor phenomena?

3. Patronage was a problem in Corinth. What might contemporary patronage relationships look like? What are some biblical guidelines for flourishing in unequal power or economic relationships?

4. Paul needed to convince the Corinthians that an over-reliance on the Roman empire was a problem. Do you think that Christians today rely on the government too much? Should Christians seek political office? What role should Christianity play in public debates over morality?

5. Paul thinks that the work of the Spirit and the development of the mind of Christ are essential if Christ-followers are going to have a salient identity. What practices are necessary for that to occur? How can we cultivate an openness to the Spirit? In what ways can the mind of Christ assist believers in overcoming problems associated with wisdom and power?

5

"YOU BELONG TO CHRIST" (3:1—4:21)

INTRODUCTION

HAVE YOU EVER STOPPED to think about how someone within the earliest Christ-movement understood their relationship to the group to which they belonged? Today, with the benefit of church history, church identities are fairly well defined, but how would someone in the first century CE have known that a person was a Christ-follower rather than a devotee to the Egyptian goddess Isis? Is this question more complicated when one considers that the Christ-movement is led by Jews and functions within the broader synagogue community? The Romans had a structured set of cultural practices that defined social relationships. Within the Christ-movement, however, people of many ethnicities and nations were being united under the lordship of Christ rather than under the domination of the empire. So

"You Belong to Christ" (3:1—4:21)

questions of belonging were crucial, and in this last part of the opening section of the letter, Paul addresses such questions by noting the way old identity structures created problems. He then offers a series of metaphors designed to construe a common ingroup identity. Finally, he develops a new ingroup prototype that contrasts with the prevailing Roman expectations for leadership and formation within the group.

HINDRANCE: OVER-IDENTIFICATION WITH OLD SOCIAL IDENTITIES (3:1-4)

There is a problem in the community with those who are primarily socially identifying with their old identities. Paul has been developing an identity-forming antithesis since 1:18, but in 3:1-4 it is applied in a different way. Up to this point, intergroup issues and boundary-marking with those outside the Christ-group have been his primary focus, but now he is interested in those living as if their identity had not been transformed. Some in the assembly had kept their old identity structures as their primary allegiance. Some of these existing identities should continue, but some will need to end, and those that do continue will require transformation. In 3:1, Paul continues to highlight the kinship of the group as he recalls for his "brother and sisters" a series of events which had occurred when he was with them: "I could not speak to you as spiritual people," that is as the prototypical group member just described in 2:12-16. He states, rather, that he had to speak to them as "people of the flesh." This subgroup had been socially identifying with key aspects of their Roman social identity, especially in their relationship to prototypical leaders, so Paul had to give them "milk" (3:2). Worse, however, is that they are still in that condition (1:12; 3:4, 22). This suggests that they were not adapting themselves to the new norms of the community, and Paul's description of them as "still of the flesh" (3:3) indicates that their ongoing behavior concerned him. Paul thinks that "jealousy and quarreling" reveal a lack of spiritual maturity (in other words, the lack of a salient in Christ social identity). In 3:4, he refocuses the Corinthians' attention back to 1:12 and reminds them that when they over-identify with a leader, they are not embodying their new life in Christ. In a significant way, 3:1–4 is the focus of Paul's message, and 3:5–23 provides the solution for the misguided sense of group belonging.

IDENTITY-FORMING METAPHORS: GOD'S FIELD, GOD'S BUILDING, AND GOD'S TEMPLE (3:5–17)

Paul asks, "What then is Apollos? What is Paul?" These questions are designed to recategorize the Corinthians' thinking and adjust the way they compare themselves to each other based on their evaluations of certain teachers within the Christ-group. Those leaders should be seen as "servants" to whom "the Lord assigned" leadership tasks (3:5). Paul then draws on agricultural images to indicate that he "planted," Apollos "watered," but "God gave the growth" (3:6). This verse presents Paul and Apollos as co-servants working in harmony with each other. Despite the conflict sometimes brought into this passage, Paul reports a conflict between the followers of these leaders, and not between the leaders themselves. Therefore, he makes it clear that no leader should be the focus of social identification within the Christ-group, repeating again his reasoning: "only God gives the growth." He recognizes that a complete end to social comparisons is not likely, so he attempts to shift the Corinthians' thinking in relation to judgment and accountability before God by continuing: "each will receive wages according to the labor of each" (3:8). Paul's point here is that socially identifying with one teacher over another indicates that one does not understand the nature of God's way of evaluating workers and reveals a lack of maturity within the community (3:1–4). In light of this, Paul states, "we are God's servants, working together." This again stresses the cooperative nature of their work though hierarchy is not fully absent (e.g., 1:4). He then describes the community as "God's field" (3:9b). They are land ready for development, a parcel that belongs to God.

Paul leaves the agricultural metaphor and shifts to one of construction when he writes that the Corinthians are also "God's building" (3:9c). The Christ-followers are a group under construction; their social world is being transformed. The imagery continues with apocalyptic language designed to maintain their social identity in ways that will facilitate mission. "The grace of God" is the focus in 3:10, especially as it relates to the practical social implications of God's work within the group (see similarly 1:4–9.) In this context, "grace" requires Paul to be engaged in a mission to the nations and requires the Corinthians to be engaged in the maintenance of that mission in Paul's absence. Continuing the construction metaphor, in 3:11, he argues that "Jesus Christ" is the community's "foundation." So, any other basis for their sense of belonging is misguided; Christ is the only way gentile alienation from the God of Israel can be overcome (1:29–31). Paul then describes a future social identity in which God will judge the work of those involved in building and maintaining the congregation (3:12–15), providing the cognitive, evaluative, and emotional resources necessary for maintaining the Corinthians' in Christ social identity. Paul does not intend to shame the Corinthians with this reminder, or to create distance between them, but to strengthen their identification with Paul and his co-workers. Later in the letter, Paul describes this communal ethos as "faith, hope, and love" (13:13).

Paul starts 3:16 by asking the Corinthian Christ-followers, "Do you not know that you are God's temple and that God's Spirit dwells in you?" Paul focuses on those who would work against the construction and maintenance of the congregation; he says "God will destroy" whoever does that (3:17a). He reminds them again that they are "God's temple" and as such should be "holy." They are God's sacred space (3:17b).[1] Paul's vision for the community relies on a metaphor that was significant in Roman Corinthian civic life. Both Roman and Greek cults were officially recognized there, especially those connected to the emperor and those that had ancient Greek roots (e.g., Apollos, Asklepius), as well as a few unique to the province (e.g., Medea).[2] This metaphor implicitly addresses the divided group identifications described in 1:12–13, showing their incompatibility with their social identity as "God's temple." In the Roman empire, sacred space existed in multiple locations: within Roman homes, outside temples, and within the broader civic structures (e.g., patronage and council meetings), which combined to produce Roman civic identity. Paul seeks, however, to situate sacred space in one location, thus transforming a key aspect of the Corinthians' civic identity. This one sacred place was positioned in the life of the community rather than in any one particular location since as "God's temple" they belong to God.

---

1. Hunt, *The Not-Very-Persecuted Church*, 76–79.
2. Bookidis, "The Sanctuaries of Corinth," 247–60.

"You Belong to Christ" (3:1—4:21)

THE GROUP BELONGING TO GOD (3:18-23)

In 3:18, Paul expresses his concern that some in the community are deceiving themselves. Their self-evaluation in terms of the unity of the group and their personal associations is mistaken. Paul again critiques those who think they are "wise in this age," picking up the earlier argument from 2:6-9 against those who rely on the political powers of his day, the Roman empire and their local collaborators. He provides a description of the type of transformation he has in mind: "become fools." Paul is calling the community to live in a way that critiques their culture, rather than following the city's civic expectations. Larry Welborn's work points out that the fool or the comic mime traditionally allows "cultural criticism" to exist safely within the empire.[3] A rejection of the world's wisdom by embracing foolishness implicitly judges the status quo and the Roman empire. In 3:19-20, Paul finally renders his verdict on the world's wisdom, reversing his terms by drawing on Israel's scriptural tradition (Job 5:13; Psalm 94:11): the "wisdom" according to which the leaders within the Christ-movement would be evaluated in the broader culture is "foolishness." In light of this, "no one should boast in human leaders" (3:21a).

Paul continues, "For all things are yours" (3:21b; Diogenes Laertius, 6.37, 72). This echoes back to his initial concern over the community's social identification with various leaders or ideologies (1:10-12), and here in 3:21-23, he addresses their lack of correct social categorization. In 3:22, he provides concrete examples of what actually belongs to the Christ-followers. "Whether Paul or Apollos or Cephas," these leaders should be understood as servants in their midst not as ideological dividing points. He then lists a series of life situations from which Greek

3. Welborn, *Paul, the Fool for Christ*, 227.

and Roman philosophical wisdom suggested detachment; even these "belong to you." Things that are significant as well as those that are morally indifferent belong to the community, but Paul does not end there. In 3:23, he writes, "and you belong to Christ and Christ belongs to God." This describes the modified hierarchical structure of identity that Paul considers necessary to reorient the Corinthians' social identity and to reinforce the Pauline mission. Christ as a fellow sibling becomes the model of a delegated submission and ownership that allows for the development of the Corinthians' social identity and furthers God's mission among the nations. The Corinthian Christ-followers had been identifying themselves with various personalities within the community and relying on the world's wisdom or ideology, but this kind of social identity had failed to produce an alternative community with a distinct ethos. Instead, it had resulted in a non-transformed voluntary association similar to those throughout the Roman Empire.[4]

SELF-EXAMINATION AND SOCIAL CATEGORIZATION IN THE CHRIST-MOVEMENT (4:1–5)

In 4:1, Paul provides specific guidance about the thought processes of the community: "Think of us this way." Giving directions for the social categorization of those within the community, he continues, "as servants of Christ" (see earlier in 3:5), "and stewards of God's mysteries," which refers back to 2:1, 7. These references to Paul's earlier discussions (3:5; 2:1, 7) reinforce the group's perception of the way Paul originally proclaimed the gospel among them. In the few years since he had founded the Christ-group in Corinth, Paul seems to have been replaced as a prototype, so he

4. Ascough, "Paul, Synagogues, and Associations," 27–52.

"You Belong to Christ" (3:1—4:21)

offers a reminder about the proper social categorization of stewards and servants. Then, in 4:2, he reestablishes a group norm by transforming their understanding of accountability: "moreover, it is required of stewards that they be found trustworthy." Such an assessment should be part of their social categorization. However, the second half of this phrase implies the possibility that a steward might not be trustworthy. Such judgment language is quite prominent in this discourse unit (see also Gal 2:17). Paul reestablishes a group norm of trustworthiness that will characterize Timothy as a group prototype in 4:17.

In 4:3, Paul's argument takes an unexpected turn. He describes the community's evaluation of himself, but he writes, "with me it is a very small matter." One might have expected Paul to emphasize the importance of the community's assessment; instead he minimizes it. He continues, "that I should be judged by you or by any human court." This describes two types of social influence and power, one which operates within the community of faith and one which is controlled by those outside (6:1–11). This discussion is clearly important to Paul since he uses the same word for "judged" twice in this verse and once in 4:5. He is providing a concrete application of his teaching in 2:14–15 that those outside the community do not have the knowledge to properly assess communal life within the Christ-movement, while those within the community of faith are not subject to the evaluation of others. However, in 4:3, Paul makes his earlier point more poignant: he does not even "judge" himself. His own self-categorizations and assessments are not trustworthy forms of evaluation either. In this one verse, Paul has called into question three of the primary means of social identity formation: the individual, in this case Paul himself; the ingroup, in this case those within the Christ-group; and the outgroup, the Roman

61

empire described by means of the law courts. Paul is not confident in any of these resources to properly assess the social implications of the gospel (2:14–15; 4:3–4). Later, Paul does temper this assertion. In 9:3 he lays out his defense for those who will examine him, and in 10:25, 27 he provides guidance for judgments concerning meat offered to idols (and adds the resources of one's "conscience"). Judgment is given a missional component in 10:27 and 14:24. There Paul guides the Corinthian Christ-followers in the way judgment about "outsiders," those who are part of a subgroup defined as "unbelievers," functions. For Paul, judgment and self-examination, what social identity describes as social categorization, are important concepts in the formation of an in-Christ identity, but they have also allowed problems to enter into the community.

In 4:4, Paul uses himself as an example and declares, "I am not aware of anything against myself." Improper self-assessments have adversely impacted communal life within the Christ-movement, so he quickly adds: "but I am not thereby acquitted." Paul recognizes that he is incapable of accurately assessing his own social involvements, and if those in the assembly follow his example, they will likely think less of their own ability to properly assess social identity practices as well. Paul then focuses the Corinthians' social categorizations upon the one in whom the community is founded: "It is the Lord who judges me." So, judgment is brought up again, and it is the "Lord" who can be relied on to properly assess their communal life. This phrase shifts the timeframe from this age to the age to come, forming identity by recontextualizing the sphere of judgment from the present social situation to a future context in which their future social identity, hopefully the one Paul seeks to create, will be evident. This apocalyptic identity discourse is even more clearly expressed in 4:5: "do not pronounce judgement before the time." The Corinthians over-identified with the political power of Rome and its present power to judge, leading them to minimize any significant role for future judgment. This is not to argue that the community had a full-blown "over-realized eschatology" (one which assumes that God's judgment is already being played out in the present) but an "over-identification with Roman imperial eschatology."[5] Paul has already expressed his lack of confidence in their ability to appropriately evaluate the social implications of the gospel (1:10–12; 2:5; 3:1, 18), so he instructs them to wait until "the Lord comes." The Lord is the only one who can accurately judge the community and its leaders, their internal motivations, categorizations, and identifications, yet rather than using this insight to demoralize the group, he reminds them that "each one will receive commendation from God." This clause reorients the temporal horizon for the congregation and adjusts the relative importance they place on their current social categorization. A transformed approach to social comparisons is part of their identity performance as they await their future "commendation from God."

PAUL'S IDENTITY, SUFFERING, AND MISSION (4:6–13)

In 4:6 Paul connects the application of his argument, which began in 3:5, to the Corinthian Christ-followers by writing, "I have applied all this to Apollos and myself for your benefit." There were no personal difficulties between Paul and Apollos, but Paul used the two of them to reveal the ingroup bias that was destabilizing the congregation. The purpose of this extended illustration is then explained: so the Corinthians might learn the meaning of the phrase,

5. Witherington, *Conflict and Community*, 295–98.

"nothing beyond what is written." However, its meaning is, in fact, disputed. It sounds like it might introduce a citation of Scripture, but no actual Scripture follows. Perhaps it refers to Paul's own writing, since in 14:37 he describes what he writes as "a command of the Lord." Whatever Paul might mean, he does add a second purpose for the illustration that is easier to understand. He wants the Corinthians to stop being "puffed up in favor of one against another." Paul's teaching here is designed to restore the community's in-Christ social identity salience by reminding them to focus on their shared identity as those called by God (1:10; 7:20–21). Paul then in 4:7 asks three rhetorical questions about the Corinthians' current practices of social categorization, all of which relate in some way to Roman patronage.[6]

In 4:8, as in 4:5, Paul is often thought to be addressing issues related to an over-realized eschatology. Perhaps, however, the Corinthians were over-identifying with Roman imperial eschatology instead. Paul begins, "Already you have all you want! Already you have become rich! Quite apart from us you have become kings!" These descriptors all reflect a positive ingroup bias as part of their social identification. Paul redeploys these categorizations to reveal their intragroup discrimination. Paul wants to reestablish the foundation of their social identity—they actually had a salient social identity, but it was misplaced. Some of them understood themselves as kings, causing them to devalue other Christ-followers. Such difficulties within the Christ-group related to the development of a patron-client social structure within the Christ-movement. This system and its role in identity formation in the broader civic culture can be seen in an inscription found in Corinth; it reads "Marcus Antonius Promachus (set up this monument to honor) his friend and patron because of his fine character

6. Clarke, *Secular and Christian Leadership*, 33.

"You Belong to Christ" (3:1—4:21)

and trustworthiness."[7] The patron-client system functioned within the context of unequal friendships and may have served as a model through which the arrogance, competition, and dissension within the congregation could have arisen. It is quite possible that the early Christ-movement developed within the framework of some form of patronage, but there is little evidence for the way it would actually have functioned, although Phlm 8–19 and Rom 16:1–2 provide some clues. Paul, in 4:8, succinctly addresses political power and patronage issues related to Roman social identity and argues that in Christ these indexes of identity should be transformed.

In 4:9–13, Paul presents a catalog of the kinds of suffering that inevitably follow the emergence of an in-Christ identity as the master social identity. Before becoming Christ-followers, members had had good relations with the broader civic community, but as they began to embody their new identity, suffering was bound to increase. So, in 4:9–10, suffering is presented as an identity-forming experience. The imagery of the condemned Roman criminals provides a story into which Christ-followers can write themselves, a narrative social identity within the context of binary social categorizations such as those listed in 4:10. Paul concludes this section by continuing the catalog of suffering in 4:10–13. He wants to move the community away from their current ingroup bias so that they will think and behave differently about the world's standards.

PAUL'S KINSHIP FORMATION (4:14–17)

In 4:14–21 Paul's identity-forming work may be described as kinship formation. The section begins in 4:14 with Paul's description of his own motives: "I am not writing this to

7. Kent, *The Inscriptions*, 107.

make you ashamed." He does not want to dominate the Corinthians or to use language like the Roman provincial collaborators, "but to admonish (*nouthetōn*) you as my beloved children." Paul's kinship language denies an attempt to shame but highlights his need to teach. The semantic range of *noutheteō* includes, as in Romans 15:14, the concept of formation, so the type of teaching that Paul has in mind is formative rather than directive. In 4:15 Paul writes that the Corinthians "might have ten thousand guardians," referring to the pedagogue, normally an older, foreign slave who walked the Roman son to school and guarded him as he developed Roman social values. Paul, however, seeks to realign the Corinthians' thinking concerning their primary kinship identification away from Roman pedagogues to him as their leader, their "father through the gospel." The concept of imitation, brought up in 4:16, was also part of the early educational experiences of Roman children as they copied famous authors not only to learn writing, but also to learn the moral values they described (Quintilian, *Orations*, 1.1.36). Paul, however, subverts Roman educational identity by shifting the focus: "be imitators of me" (see also 4:6). Concepts related to education continue in 4:17 where Paul brings up his role as a teacher. A teacher often acted as a father, and thus his instructions to his students can be understood as kinship formation (Epictetus, *Discourses*, 3.22.81–82). Paul, however, by presenting himself as a teacher, substitutes his own guidance for the wisdom taught in Roman schools, sometimes by Greeks (2:16).

Paul offers another solution for the competing identity narratives in 4:17: "For this reason I sent you Timothy." Timothy, whom Paul had sent to Ephesus but who was back with Paul at the time of his writing (16:10), was uniquely qualified to help guide the Corinthians through the changing circumstances of life in Christ. He would serve as

"You Belong to Christ" (3:1—4:21)

another prototypical member for the group. Paul, in 4:14, had already described the Corinthians as "my beloved children." Now he describes Timothy with similar kinship language: "my beloved and faithful child in the Lord," and for Paul, this Lord is Christ, not Caesar. He relies on the resources of social memory and Jewish teaching discourse as he describes the reason for Timothy's coming, "to remind you of my ways in Christ Jesus." Paul had preached the gospel to them, had written them a previous letter, but they had misunderstood Paul's message.[8] Thus, Paul speaks through Timothy to affect their socio-cultural practices. He then rhetorically connects the Christ-group in Corinth with the superordinate group, members of the Christ-movement throughout the Roman empire (16:1–4). When Paul writes, "as I teach them everywhere in every church," he not only establishes his own function within the Christ-movement, but also the kinship formation that, as discussed above, was inherent in a teaching role. These connections to the broader community of followers of Christ show that Paul's mission strategy for the Corinthians requires them to detach their primary social identity from the broader Corinthian community and see themselves primarily as members of the larger body of Christ. By reprioritizing their existing Roman social identifications, Paul supports the formation of a common Corinthian mission; his goal is an alternative community with a distinct ethos.

PAUL'S EMPOWERMENT OF THE COMMUNITY (4:18–21)

In 4:18 Paul begins this section by saying, "some (*tines*) of you, thinking that I am not coming to you, have become arrogant." Verses 18–21 are often understood as an example of

8. Fairclough, *Discourse and Change*, 63–73.

a discourse of domination. However, by using an indefinite pronoun (*tines*), Paul raises concerns about arrogant behavior without publically shaming the offending members. The Greek word used for "arrogant" here is rare outside of the New Testament, but it does occur in Herodas, *Mime*, 2.32, describing those who are arrogant based on their birth (see 1:26). A small subgroup within the congregation, then, may have been priding themselves on their "noble birth." If so, they would have been identifying primarily with aspects of their Roman educational social identity rather than with their identity in Christ. This theme of cultural boasting occurs throughout this letter, and in each case Paul argues that those aspects of a Christ-follower's identity need transformation. For example, 4:6, 18, 19 suggest that some had become arrogant because of their greater educational achievements; 5:1–2 indicates that Roman views of masculinity had marred sexual identity and group norms, and 8:1 illustrates differences within the Corinthian assembly that arose based on a Roman ethos concerning a continued relationship to idols. Paul's alternative ethos is introduced in 8:1 with the phrase, "knowledge puffs up, but love builds up," and in 13:4 he writes, "love is not boastful or arrogant." Paul's concern for arrogance within the community is really a concern with power discourse—the site at which he rejects Roman cultural norms. Boasting is an area in which existing identities do not continue in Christ.

Paul shifts the discourse from reported speech to first person speech and provides a firmer assessment of their attitude: "But I will come to you soon, if the Lord wills." Then he describes how he intends to address the situation when he does arrive: "I will find out not the talk of these arrogant people but their power" (4:19). Paul is reestablishing who is part of the ingroup (those with power) and who properly belongs to the outgroup (those with only talk). As

"You Belong to Christ" (3:1—4:21)

he does throughout 1 Corinthians 1–4, Paul is providing the Corinthian Christ-followers with the knowledge they need to understand and apply the social implications of the gospel. Social identity theory claims that an individual's self-concept comes from his or her perceived membership within a social group. Self-categorization theory further argues that, once this ingroup identity is established, outgroup stereotyping occurs. This strengthens one's identification with the ingroup, making that identity salient. Paul does that here, using outgroup language, calling those with only talk "arrogant." He redefines their identification categories from their "talk" to their "power."

Paul's apocalyptic worldview provides the foundation for his kinship formation: "For the kingdom of God depends not on talk but on power" (4:20). This anti-imperial polemic reminds the Christ-followers who have put their trust in the Roman "kingdom" that in comparison to God's "kingdom," it is not very powerful after all. In Romans 14:16, one of the few other places where Paul uses the phrase "the kingdom of God," he similarly redefines the nature of God's kingdom as compared to that of Rome. Paul rarely uses kingdom language, however, because of the possibility of its being misunderstood in the context of Roman imperial ideology.

Paul ends the section in 4:21 with a question: "What would you prefer?" Paul's rhetoric of empowerment offers his hearers two options. First, he asks "Am I to come to you with a stick?" What type of stick is in view? Proverbs 22:15 may form the substructure of Paul's rhetoric here because, like the Corinthians passage, it contains significant kinship formation language (such as "boy" and "discipline"). The synthetic parallelism of the proverb begins: "Folly is bound up in the heart of a boy," and it concludes, "but the rod of discipline drives it far away." Paul's kinship formation required more than Martial's "sinister rod" or the "scepter" from a Roman teacher (*Epigrams*, 10.62.10; see 4:15); it required a stick of training (4:21). Though a stick is mentioned, Paul's main purpose is not to threaten the Corinthians with physical violence. He is actually speaking out against violent Roman imperial polemic. He is saying: "In light of all I have just said, would you want me to come to you as a Roman teacher," in other words with a stick, or "with love in a spirit of gentleness?" You decide. By putting the Corinthian Christ-followers in charge of their choice, even this ending expresses some empowerment and transformation rather than total domination. Paul concludes this section by introducing the way he intends to define the ingroup later in chapter 13—by an ethos of love and an ethic of humility (2 Cor 10:1).

DISCUSSION QUESTIONS

1. The Corinthians were continuing to identify with their old identity structures. How might that still happen today? There are some aspects of a person's identity that continue and should be cultivated within Christian communities. How can you distinguish between those that are incompatible and those that are compatible with an in Christ social identity?

2. Do you think that the community as God's temple suggests that Christian identity is primarily individual or corporate? What benefits arise from thinking about Christian identity primarily as a corporate one?

3. Paul thinks that a renewed awareness that we belong to God is crucial for spiritual maturity. How would your identity and lifestyle change if you allowed that truth to prioritize your cultural engagements? How

"You Belong to Christ" (3:1—4:21)

would you reprioritize your time? How would you think about areas that are morally indifferent? What does it mean for you to recognize that you belong to Christ?

4. Paul warns the Corinthians not to overestimate their ability to assess themselves properly. Do you struggle with this? If so, what might contribute to this problem? How might this be overcome?

5. Paul contends that cultural boasting is an identity performance that should not continue in Christ. Do you agree? What areas of your cultural identity are you proud of? What are some negative possibilities associated with this identity? What are the positive ones?

6

"THE BODY FOR THE LORD" (5:1—7:40)

INTRODUCTION

When it comes to sexuality, Paul has a bad reputation. He is said to have tried to restrict human freedom and impose rigorous guidelines that reinforced existing power structures in the Roman empire. Is such a view warranted? Is Paul truly a champion of traditional sexual, gender, and marriage values? This chapter wrestles with these questions and, along the way, looks at examples of existing social identities that were sometimes transformed and sometimes remained unchanged within the Christ-movement. Paul's instructions in this section about the way Christ-followers should embody their renewed life in the Lord encourages the reader, both ancient and contemporary, to envision new ways to allow Scripture and tradition to inform their life together. For Paul, the body is for the Lord, and that

"The Body for the Lord" (5:1—7:40)

ownership makes certain claims on our lives both for our flourishing and for his mission in the world. Paul begins by addressing identity performances he deems problematic; then he offers guidance on marriage as well as his rule in all the churches. Finally, he concludes this section with a discussion of secondary gender identities and the nature of freedom in Christ.

PROBLEM: EXISTING SEXUAL IDENTITY (5:1–13)

Paul, in 5:1—11:1, instructs the Corinthians on what it means to embody a new set of ethical practices. He begins by addressing behaviors that should result from having the mind of Christ. In 5:1 Paul writes, "It is actually reported that there is sexual immorality (*porneia*) among you." He is pointing out to the Corinthians that he has received an oral report about this situation that they had not mentioned in the letter they wrote to him. He continues, "and of a kind that is not found even among pagans." This comparison with pagans, especially when combined with the involvement of the Corinthian Christ-followers in their broader civic community, may indicate that those outside the group are aware of this behavior. Together, these suggest that the Christ-group's social identity is at stake since their standing within the broader community is in jeopardy.[1] Paul's idea of mission as social identification requires just such involvement, but in this instance their speech did not match their behavior. He engages in an intergroup comparison by noting that this specific "sexual immorality," where "a man is living with his father's wife," does not occur even among the pagan nations. If Paul expected such a comparison to be effective, some of the Corinthian Christ-followers must have cared about that outgroup, and thus were identifying socially with

1. May, *The Body for the Lord*, 60.

Roman sexual identity. Paul uses stereotypes about the nations' sexual deviance as a negative foil for the Corinthians' ethical behavior (Deut 12:29–31; 1 Kgs 14:24). In this case a Christ-follower is having sex with his step-mother, which itself would be a violation of Roman law (Gaius, *Institutes*, 1.63). Paul indicates they had become "arrogant," assuming, for example, that even Roman sexual laws no longer applied to them, while they should have instead "removed" the person from the group (5:2). As an engineer of identity, Paul lays out what he expects the group to do, "hand this man over to Satan." He wants to mobilize the Corinthians to reshape their social reality. Although Paul appears punitive, his instruction is only directed at the man, the one who has the power in this situation. Furthermore, Paul's goal is that the man's "spirit may be saved in the day of the Lord" (5:3–5). Paul has already mentioned cultural boasting as an area where gentile identity does not continue in Christ (1:10–12, 28–29, 31; 3:5, 21), and here Paul returns to this underlying problem, "your boasting is not a good thing" (5:6). He then offers a parable dealing with "leaven" that relates to an unscriptural thought pattern inherited from the Corinthians' previous social identifications (5:7). The omission of leaven in the baking instructions in Exod 12:8 broke with existing Egyptian social practices, and here Paul prompts a break with their existing attitude toward "sexual immorality" (5:1).

Paul describes "Christ" as the "paschal lamb" and encourages the congregation to "celebrate the festival" (5:7b–8). This is often taken only as a metaphor but in light of 16:8 one should not set aside the possibility that Paul, as well as the Corinthian Christ-followers, celebrated the Passover. Even Philo could use the Passover meal in figurative ways but still participate in an actual meal (Philo, *On the Special Laws*, 2.145). The Christ-movement is still part of the

"The Body for the Lord" (5:1—7:40)

synagogue community, and, for Paul, Israel's ritual life continues to be relevant. At the same time, as an "impresario of identity," he is creating a new ritual life for gentiles to relate to the God of Israel as gentiles (7:17–24; 11:23–32).[2]

Paul next clarifies his earlier written instructions concerning separation from the broader "world" (5:9–10). Although, as we have seen, some Corinthians were identifying so closely with those outside the group that their behavior was not changing enough, others thought that Paul's instructions meant avoiding outsiders altogether (v. 10). Paul, however, is not inclined to "judge those outside," leaving that to "God" (5:12–13). He is instead concerned with the "immoral" and "idolaters" within the group (5:11–12) and wants to bring about ethical changes among them: "Drive out the wicked person" (5:13). For Paul, the holiness of the community is crucial. Social identity approaches argue that groups require positive self-evaluation against an outgroup. The negative outgroup evaluation results in a positive ingroup identity, but in this case the "immoral brother" is an ingroup member with worse-than-outgroup behavior associated with his sexual identity. Paul has again undermined the Corinthians' confidence in their ability to assess the ingroup correctly, and their failure provides more evidence that they need to develop "the mind of Christ" (2:16; 3:1–4; 4:3). Paul also needs them to understand properly what separation from the "world" requires since he expects them to engage in mission as social identification, an approach to existing identities that sees them as missionally significant. Christ-movement members function as mediators between those "being saved" and those "perishing" (1:18; 10:33b). Paul describes this type of life in 5:9–10 and 10:31—11:1. Such a performance of identity

2. Haslam, Reicher, and Platow, *The New Psychology of Leadership*, 171–92.

causes no offense among outsiders (10:32). It adjusts civic practices enough to cause them to ask questions (10:28). It alters ritual observances with outsiders in view (14:23), and it stays in relationship with outsiders whose ethical practices differ from those on the inside (5:9–10). Paul puts social identity to work within the Christ-movement; this approach to ingroup membership can be described as mission as social identification (see also 1 Thess 4:11–12; Phil 4:5).

PROBLEM: OVER-RELIANCE ON ROMAN LEGAL IDENTITY (6:1–11)

Paul indicates that he has also learned that some of the Christ-followers were taking other members to the local civil magistrates; he concludes that this was shameful (6:1, 5–6). Paul's negative assessment of the Roman legal system is quite a severe critique since their claim that the gods had destined them to rule the world, particularly the barbarians, was based on their ability to govern according to Roman law (Virgil, *Aeneid*, 1.286–96).[3] Paul categorizes the judges as "unbelievers" and defines them as those "who have no standing in the church" (6:4, 6). The boundary Paul sets between Christ-followers and the Roman legal system is further supported by his apocalyptic ideology: Christ-followers should be able to judge these "trivial cases" since one day they "will judge the world" and "angels" (6:2–3). Paul addresses their present social identity by evaluating their local engagement with the Roman civic authorities in relation to their future social identity in Christ. He concludes by reminding them, using an early baptismal formula, of the primary reason for not going to those outside the Christ-movement for justice: They have been "washed,

3. Tucker, *You Belong to Christ*, 104–5.

"The Body for the Lord" (5:1—7:40)

sanctified, and justified in the name of the Lord and in the Spirit of our God" (6:11). The use of an early baptism formula is important because identity formation is embedded in rituals, and early Christ-movement rituals served to reinforce the boundaries for the community.

Paul continues to reshape identity in 6:8, "But you yourselves wrong and defraud—and believers at that." He is not against Roman law in general but against the way patrons, who provided protection for clients in the Roman courts, were also protecting their clients from ingroup members they had wronged. Thus, Paul is using ingroup and outgroup language to lay the foundation for a new identity. In 6:8–9, he argues that *they*, the Christ-followers, are "wrongdoers"; then he goes on to question their membership in the "kingdom of God," since they are engaging in such quarrelsome legal practices. While his argument continues in 6:10–11, he punctuates it in 6:8 with the hope that his audience will end their current practice of taking those within the community of Christ-followers before the local magistrates, if they properly understand their identity. (On some of the other practices in 6:9–10, see below.)

The end of the textual unit is central to an identity-critical analysis of this passage. In 6:11, Paul calls to mind the Corinthians' former identity: "And this is what some of you used to be." This reminds the Christ-followers not only of their previous identity, but also of the ways it has and has not already changed, promoting the elements of future change that Paul is suggesting. In this section, Paul is not only concerned about proper procedure for resolving disputes. He is establishing a particular ethos of identity that requires certain boundaries, and he negotiates them through his rhetoric. This identity will allow for a more stable community and promote mission in Roman Corinth.

By going before the local magistrates, the Corinthians were in effect admitting that their identity had not changed. Paul reminds the Christ-followers that this was shameful and, echoing an earlier argument, that they were not as wise as they appeared (6:5). If the Corinthians are transformed in Christ, this should show in their interactions with the civic authorities, as well as with one another. Paul, it may be argued, is engaging in apocalyptic identity formation. He reminds the Corinthians that they are transformed in Christ and thus members of the kingdom of God; that transformation and membership should reveal itself in the way they interact with others for the purpose of extending the Pauline mission (1:8).

SOLUTION: CHRIST-LIKE EMBODIMENT (6:12–20)

To solve the problems associated with existing sexual identities (5:1–13) and an over-reliance on Roman law (6:1–11), Paul offers a vision for a new way to embody the Corinthians' identity, one that is Christ-like (6:12–20). Paul begins by quoting what is likely a Corinthian slogan: "All things are lawful for me" (6:12; see also 10:23), a view he disagrees with since certain ethical practices do not align with an in-Christ identity (5:1–8; 6:9–11). So he then corrects it: "but not all things are beneficial." He repeats the slogan again and then states "but I will not be dominated by anything." He is not concerned about the rights of Christ-followers but the possible ruin that a misuse of their freedom could cause. Paul then quotes another slogan: "Food is meant for the stomach and the stomach for food" (6:13). This suggests that some in Corinth had come to think that the way they embodied their in Christ identity in temporary, everyday details like food did not actually matter. Paul

"The Body for the Lord" (5:1—7:40)

agrees to a certain extent; however, he does distinguish between sex and food. The latter is eschatologically unimportant but the former is crucial. Since "the body is for the Lord," it must not be used for sexual immorality (6:13). What one does with the body in relation to sex "goes to the root of who the believer is."[4] Paul therefore again affects the Christ-followers' present identity by constructing a future social identity that connects the Lord's resurrection with the Christ-followers' future bodily resurrection (6:14).

For Paul, Christ-like embodiment is possible since Christ-followers' "bodies are members of Christ" and have been "united to the Lord" (6:15, 17). Union with Christ is not primarily a doctrine to be believed but a pattern of life to be lived, in Christ, by the work of the Spirit. Thus, to be in Christ is a social identity, one that cannot coexist with "sexual immorality" generally or with sex with a "prostitute" specifically (6:16). The NRSV suggests that Paul's alternative vision to the Corinthians' current sexual status quo is to "shun fornication (*porneia*)" (6:18), but this translation is too broad. The context suggests that Paul is specifically, as in 6:13 and 7:2, urging them to "shun sex with prostitutes." That being the case, the earlier use of *pornoi* "fornicators" in 6:9 likely refers to this narrower form of sexual immorality. In 6:18, Paul actually labels an individual who engages in such practices as "the fornicator (*ho porneuōn*)," using the term to inscribe a deviant subgroup identity on this segment of the Christ-group.

Paul continues his approach to this subject by asking, "Do you not know that your body is a temple of the Holy Spirit within you?" (6:19). Here the corporate aspect of the temple metaphor is applied to individual Christ-followers. Self-categorization theory argues that once a person sees herself as a member of a particular group, she begins to

4. May, *The Body of the Lord*, 110.

evaluate herself based on the norms of that group. Paul seems to be counting on such a process when he creates a rhetorical space for a righteous kingdom that calls each Corinthian Christ-follower to sacrificial holiness and righteousness in his daily life. This embodying of sacred space provides the cognitive information necessary for understanding the nexus of Paul's corporate and individual use of temple imagery. This use, when the individual aspect is brought to the fore, connects with another metaphor that is important when dealing with contested ritual space—the body of Christ (6:15). Paul conceives of the Christ-group (*ekklēsia*) as ritual space, as embodied temple space. To be a Christ-follower is to be a member of the body of Christ, not a person primarily identified as an individual. Paul, however, still holds the individual responsible for the behavior that flows from a transformed identity (6:18). Paul's conclusion is that each individual body within the community of Christ-followers functions as a temple of God, a nested identity within the larger community as temple (3:16–17) and body (12:12–14), and thus they should "glorify God" with their bodies (6:19–20). Individual differences continue within this one body, but domination is not to be a part of it (12:13; Gal 3:28).

PROBLEM: MARRIAGE AND PRE-CHRIST-FOLLOWING RELATIONS (7:1–16)

Paul begins this new section by writing "now concerning (*peri de*) the matters about which you wrote." This discourse marker occurs throughout the letter to introduce Paul's responses to the issues the Corinthians has raised. Paul summarizes their position in the slogan, "It is well for a man not to touch a woman," but the point was apparently debated. Therefore, Paul offers his perspective on

"The Body for the Lord" (5:1—7:40)

this important social identity issue: "each man should have his own wife and each woman her own husband." It may seem that Paul is wholeheartedly supporting marriage, but his support is designed to solve a more pressing problem, avoiding "sexual immorality (*porneia*)." This concern is probably why he initially focuses only on conjugal rights, both in 7:3 and in his broader statement in 7:4 that there ought to be relational mutuality between the husband and wife. This development, novel within the Roman cultural setting, would contribute to the emergence of a distinct ethos among the Christ-followers. Paul expects that human sexuality will find expression within the holy and mission-oriented ethos he wants to develop within the Christ-following community, but, in accord with this ethos, he also suggests that a couple might temporarily refrain from that expression to prioritize "prayer." This, however, should occur only by mutual consent and for a brief amount of time "because of your lack of self-control" (7:5). Paul's conclusion about this temporary suspension of sexual relations is interesting from a social identity leadership perspective: "This I say by way of concession, not of command" (7:6). Paul does not lead with a command to which he expects obedience; rather, he recognizes that marriage embeds the partners into a new social identity that has its own culturally defined identity performances that create cross-cutting relational difficulties where it conflicts with other, previously established identities.

Furthermore, when it comes to marriage, Paul is not a strong ingroup prototype since he was not married and had not established the proper Roman household that would have been the norm in Corinth (9:5). He puts himself forward only for those Corinthians who, like him, have celibacy as "a particular gift from God," which, at the same time, he desires for all (7:7). In fact, when Paul offers his guidance to those in the community who are not married, "the unmarried and the widows," he wants them to "remain unmarried" (7:8). Both groups are identifiable social identity groupings in Corinth. Those that are unmarried include both genders (7:8, 11, 32, 34), but he also specifically mentions the female "virgin" (7:25, 28, 34, 36, 37). Since Paul identifies the virgins as a subgroup of the unmarried, and since he later mentions "widows" as well (7:8; see also 1 Tim 5:3–16), gender identity among the Christ-following Corinthians seems to have included both primary (married and unmarried) and secondary gender identities (virgins and widows).[5] The unmarried are to stay within those subgroup identities unless they have been called to marriage (7:9).

Paul next offers direction to those who are married, although he primarily focuses on issues of divorce. Situations where the marriage occurred before one spouse joined the Christ-following movement are particularly difficult from the standpoint of identity formation. Paul is convinced that marriage ought to be permanent, but he also recognizes the reality of divorce (7:10, 15). In such cases, is remarriage an acceptable option? After describing the contagious nature of holiness in 7:14, Paul presents a situation in which an "unbelieving partner separates." In that instance, the remaining spouse is "not bound" (7:15). Thus, remarriage seems to be an option; however, 7:11 seems to move in the opposite direction. If there is a separation, the "wife" should "remain unmarried or else be reconciled to her husband." The difference in options may relate to the legitimacy of the divorce (7:15; cf. Matt 5:32; 19:9). Perhaps 7:11 addresses an illegitimate divorce in which a remarriage should not occur, but if the separation is legitimate then remarriage may be considered (7:10–11). Paul, however, ends his marriage

5. Collins, *All but Invisible*, forthcoming.

halakah, his ethical ruling, by suggesting that it may be better to remain in the relationship since the unbelieving partner might be saved through the spouse's continuing social influence (7:16). Through these suggestions, Paul is reordering the Christ-followers' identity hierarchy so that even an otherwise separate social identity, marriage, may be part of the Christ-group's collective action.

SOLUTION: REMAIN IN YOUR CALLING (7:17–24)

Paul's "rule in all the churches," his halakah, is that Christ-followers are to live according to the call of God (7:17). The NRSV translation, "let each of you lead the life that the Lord has assigned, to which God has called you," gives the impression that Paul has a "state," "social condition," or "vocation" in mind, and some interpreters have concluded that Paul rejects all social or legal status changes or identity transformations for followers of Christ. Part of the problem is that interpreters often think that the words "assigned" (*emerisen*) and "called" (*keklēken*) are near synonyms and, because 7:20–24 also discusses "call," they bring the meaning of "assigned" into these verses as well. However, the two terms refer to different aspects of the Christ-followers' identity. The first, "assigned," refers to all the various life practices that result from different spiritual gifts. (Similarly, the "gift" in 7:7 results in a different "manner" of life; Rom 12:3.) The second, "called," as it is used in 7:17, 20, 21, is an interior call to be in Christ. Paul's "rule" concerns who a person considers themselves to be. For Paul, being in Christ is the superordinate identity which deprioritizes all other indexes of identity. However, some of the Corinthians were giving up this new identity in Christ when they prioritized key aspects of their Roman social identity. This, as Scott

Bartchy suggests, indicates that Paul's earliest opposition came mostly from those who saw that his gospel would get in the way of the kinship, loyalty, economic, gender, and social patterns already in place. In such situations, the pressure to not remain in their calling with God must have been intense.[6]

Calling does not erase all other identities, yet it does re-orient social life. Ethnic identity indexes such as "circumcision" and "uncircumcision" do not disappear, but their importance is reprioritized (7:18). Thus, Paul teaches the community to continue to identify with the ethnic group they belonged to when they begin to follow Christ. Both Jewish and non-Jewish ethnic identities continue as valid expressions of life in Christ; this is what is meant by a particularistic approach to Christ-movement social identity (10:32).[7] Paul does not ask the community to stop the practices that fit their ethnic identity; he simply reminds them that "obeying the commandments of God" (7:19; Gal 5:6, 6:15) must come first.

The NRSV continues, "Let each of you remain in the condition (*klēsis*) in which you were called" (7:20). The Greek word *klēsis* would be better translated as "calling." Thus, Paul is saying Christ-followers should remain in the *calling in Christ* into which they were called. The calling in view here is the call of God through Christ to be in Christ. This verse, then, does not sanctify the social status quo nor suggest that a person is called to be a slave or to remain as one. In 7:21, Paul is concerned about the social implications of the gospel for slaves. Bartchy's translation is helpful: "Were you a slave when you were called? Don't worry about it. But if, indeed, you become manumitted, by all means

---

6. Bartchy, *Paulus hat nicht gelehrt*, 234, 237.
7. Tucker, *Remain in Your Calling*, 62–88.

"The Body for the Lord" (5:1—7:40)

[as a freedman/woman] live according to God's calling."[8] His point here is that even if you can gain your freedom and thus a new status, it is still God's call that defines your identity. This applies to the social implications of his gospel for all the examples of social identities in 7:1–40. In earlier passages he challenged those aspects of Roman social life that were getting in the way of the salience of an in Christ social identity. Now, he addresses an aspect of Roman social life that some thought could adversely affect one's relationship with God: slavery. Paul transforms the social stigma of slavery so that it becomes an index, metaphorical or otherwise, of an in-Christ identity within the Christ-movement (7:22–23). All Christ-followers, therefore, even those with differences that remain, should be accepted because all share the same interior call. Paul concludes his discussion with the reminder: In "whatever" calling "you were called, brothers and sisters, there remain with God" (7:24).

PROBLEM: SECONDARY GENDER IDENTITIES (7:25–40)

Paul picks up his earlier discussion by writing "now concerning virgins." For Paul, the category "female" would be classified as a primary gender identity while "virgin" (or "widow") would be a secondary one. This further suggests that what contemporary gender theorists refer to as orientation may have some points of connection with Paul's thinking on gender.[9] He continues to offer his halakic ruling on the question the Corinthians raised since he was unaware of any teaching from the Jesus tradition on this topic (7:25). As in the earlier part of the chapter, Paul does not fossil-

8. Bartchy, *Paulus hat nicht gelehrt*, 238–39.

9. Cobb, *Dying to be Men*, 18–32. Cobb applies social identity theory to gender and Christian identity.

ize Christ-movement identity by validating the status quo. His overarching principle is that Christ-followers are "not bound." They have freedom, but they are called to peace (7:15). Paul expects change, for example, when he offers guidance to a couple struggling with desire, telling them to marry (7:28–36). On the one hand, Paul does not encourage the Corinthians to follow the example of Christ and remain single without establishing a Roman household; however, he does applaud those who "refrain" from marriage, since he sees that as a "better" path (7:37–38). In 7:39 Paul writes, "a wife is bound as long as her husband lives" but after the death of the spouse the situation changes. In that case, "she is free to marry . . . only in the Lord." This instruction recognizes the presence of another secondary gender identity (a married woman) and offers a halakah for how it could be construed, a halakah that is in line with latter rabbinic teaching in Mishnah *Gittin* 9:3. He concludes with the reminder that the woman would be better to "remain as she is" (7:40), in her calling in Christ. Thus, throughout this chapter, Paul emphasizes that regardless of any identity transformations that might occur, each one should remain in his or her calling in Christ, into which he or she was called (7:17, 20, 24).[10]

DISCUSSION QUESTIONS

1. Paul needed to correct the Corinthians' understanding of separation from the world. What is your current view of separation from those who do not follow Christ? Why do many within the church resist cultural engagement? What does mission as social identification look like in your cultural setting?

10. Bartchy, *Paulus hat nicht gelehrt*, 237–38.

"The Body for the Lord" (5:1—7:40)

2. Does 1 Corinthians 6:1–11 mean that Christians should not take each other to court today? Should churches ever be involved in the court system? Is arbitration a better option for the resolution of civil infractions? Are these verses limited to civil and economic concerns rather than criminal cases? Does Romans 13:1–7 help apply Paul's teaching about criminal cases?

3. Paul has to instruct the free Corinthian males to stop having sex with prostitutes, a behavior that was culturally acceptable. What sexual practices are deemed morally neutral in our culture that need a similar critique? How is one's sexual identity relevant in Christ, or is it?

4. Paul offers competing guidelines about divorce and remarriage. How can one begin to develop a consistent stance on this in light of Paul's varying directives? Is Paul's guidance on marriage and divorce tied to his culture? How do you know?

5. Paul's rule is that one should continue to identify with their existing ethnic and social identities in Christ. Are there any limits to this? How can Paul's rule work in a multiethnic church setting? What are some potential challenges in trying to live out Paul's rule?

7

"DO EVERYTHING FOR THE GLORY OF GOD" (8:1—11:1)

INTRODUCTION

IN 1823, REV. DR. Richard Furman, the President of the Baptist State Convention, wrote to John Wilson, the Governor of South Carolina to request a "day of public humiliation and thanksgiving" because he saw the hand of God in the way both a slave rebellion had been avoided, and a hurricane had caused much suffering. At the end of his letter, he concludes "that the holding of slaves is justifiable by the doctrine and example contained in Holy writ; and is therefore consistent with Christian uprightness, both in sentiment and conduct." He argues that the state should restrain and punish cruelty to slaves, and that masters have a duty "to grant religious privileges to those who desire them

"Do Everything for the Glory of God" (8:1—11:1)

and furnish proper evidence of their sincerity and uprightness." After all, he notes, "the salvation of men is intimately connected with the glory of their God and Redeemer."[1]

Claiming that what a group does is for the glory of God is generally thought of as a means of political domination and conformity. It is quite striking how often Furman refers to the good of the community in his letter. The widespread normalization of this sinful behavior in the United States may come between today's interpreters and the text and cause Paul's instructions to be misunderstood. However, Paul frames his advice more narrowly, as a way to define the Corinthians relative to those outside the group while also addressing competing visions of identity inside the group. He covers such topics as idol food, rights and responsibilities, mission as social identification, self-discipline, the discontinuance of certain identities, the role of Scripture in identity formation, and the importance of proper embodiment in Christ.

PROBLEM: FOOD OFFERED TO IDOLS AND CIVIC ENGAGEMENT (8:1–13)

Problems associated with food and the table had contributed to disunity within the community. The Corinthians wrote to Paul to clarify several related ethical issues that were part of the everyday lived experience in Corinth. In 8:1, Paul writes, "now concerning" (*peri de*) which is the third time he uses this literary marker to refer to the contents of the letter the Corinthians had written to him (7:1, 25). In 8:1–13 and 10:14–22, Paul addresses the Corinthians' participation in civic meals, likely at one of the Roman temples in the colony, for example, the dining rooms attached to

1. Furman, *Exposition of the Views*, 20, 24.

the Asklepieion.[2] In 10:23—11:1 he discusses food from the marketplace and in the household of a non-Christ-follower while in 11:17–34 he addresses table fellowship within the Christ-movement. In each case, meals are involved, but sometimes the issue is related to a specific food, and sometimes the meal itself is in question.

When Paul writes about "food sacrificed to idols" (8:1), he does not immediately criticize the Corinthians' practice. He recognizes that those who have asked this question do have "knowledge." He agrees with them that none of the deities represented at the various shrines, in fact, "no idol in the world really exists." Further, the Corinthians are correct that "there is no God but one." This phrase in 8:4 and in 8:6 is an allusion to the *Shema*, which was central to the Jewish worldview (Deut 6:4). Their knowledge, therefore, was correctly aligned with their in Christ social identity. However, their application of this knowledge was contributing to some of the problems within the relational web of the community, particularly "eating in the temple of an idol" (8:10). From the point of view of those who had knowledge, they were not participating in the worship of a deity since no other gods exist. Yet others within the group disagreed. Social identity includes both knowledge and motivating emotions; the Corinthian Christ-followers that Paul is addressing had accurate knowledge but were deficient at the emotional level. Paul's primary concern in this passage is not to debate idolatry but to raise the emotionally-laden question of what happens to fellow Christ-followers who do not have the same knowledge and who might be "encouraged to the point of eating food sacrificed to idols" (8:7, 10). Even reclining in a temple of an idol like Asklepios is a "sin" for Paul since it can have devastating effects on other group members (8:11–12). As an entrepreneur of identity,

2. Fotopoulos, *Food offered to Idols*, 59–63.

"Do Everything for the Glory of God" (8:1—11:1)

he then puts himself forward as a group prototype (8:13). Paul abstains from eating food he knows is permitted so that he will not confuse a fellow Christ-follower and tempt them to commit idolatry.[3]

The cognitive and emotional aspects of the group must be kept in mind when it comes to eating in the temple of a deity, but Paul does not think primarily in terms of individuals, but in terms of his concern for the holiness of the community. The actions of those who have knowledge threaten that holiness. For Paul, the most important issue is a behavior that injures another Christ-follower by encouraging them to weaken their exclusive loyalty to the God of Israel (8:11; Rom 14:15). Paul concludes in 8:12 that "when you thus sin against members of your family, and wound their conscience when it is weak, you sin against Christ." The close connection Paul envisions between fellow Christ-followers and Christ himself shows up again later in 12:27 when he describes the community as "the body of Christ." They are to embody holiness (1:2) and are corporately defined as "God's temple" which is also "holy" (3:16–17). So, in 8:1–13 Paul argues that the Corinthians should not participate in public temple meals because a fellow Christ-follower may misinterpret their behavior. Seeing them eating "food offered to idols" may encourage them to participate in idolatry. This would jeopardize the holiness of the community by drawing them back to this past social identification as an idol worshipper, an identity that should no longer describe those in Christ (12:2).

---

3. Ehrensperger, *Paul and the Crossroads of Cultures*, 189–209.

SOLUTION: BALANCE BETWEEN GOSPEL-INFORMED RIGHTS AND RESPONSIBILITIES (9:1-18)

Paul puts himself forward as one who understands the balance between the rights one has in Christ and the responsibilities that come from one's "work in the Lord," in other words, his mission efforts to take the gospel to the nations (9:1). Often chapter 9 is thought to be a digression where Paul defends his apostleship (9:2-3); it seems to fit awkwardly between chapters 8 and 10. However, Paul is more likely writing about rights (9:4-6) and about what should be given up to keep from becoming an "obstacle in the way of the gospel of Christ" (9:12). As this principle is applied in 8:1—11:1, it shows that Christ-followers have a responsibility, in their various identity performances related to idol food or civic entanglements, never to become a "stumbling block to the weak" (8:9), nor to "cause one of them to fall" (8:13), nor to "give offense" to others (10:32). From this perspective, in chapter 9, Paul is reestablishing his leadership position to address a perceived shift in the ingroup prototype, especially as it relates to mission as social identification (8:13). He needs to position himself as a leader for the Corinthians so that later in the letter he can offer his recommendations for the maintenance of their in Christ social identity.

In 9:3-18, Paul addresses those who have determined to "examine" him, likely a small group of imperial or provincial elites (9:3). He makes it clear that he has a "right" to receive financial support for his gospel mission and highlights the practice of "other apostles, the brothers of the Lord, and Cephas" (9:4-6). He compiles a series of integrated illustrations to argue his claim for material support (9:7-14). These illustrations consist of cultural images of various identity performances, such as those "working,"

"Do Everything for the Glory of God" (8:1—11:1)

"doing military service," "temple service," farming, and "athletes," that link familiar identities to the social identity Paul is negotiating. Embedded within these arguments is a reference to the "law," specifically "the law of Moses" (9:8–9). Paul cites Deut 25:4 to establish that those who labor for the gospel have the right to be supported by those who benefit from such labor. Paul seems then to reject Moses's authority since he does not receive financial support from the Corinthians. However, he later (9:14–15) also seems to reject a similar teaching from the "Lord" on this topic (one that was eventually recorded in Luke 10:7), yet he clearly does not reject the Lord's authority over his life, identity, and mission. Moses's authority, too, then, as recorded in Torah, continues to be an authorizing discourse for Paul, embedded as he is within Judaism, even in his mission to the nations (7:19; 9:21). He concludes by reminding the Corinthians that he proclaims the "gospel free of charge" and does not "make full use of" his "rights in the gospel" (9:18). This is the model of behavior that he wants them to follow about idol food and civic entanglements.

Paul's approach in Corinth ensures that he is not a burden to those living at or near subsistence level, likely the majority of the congregation (1:24–26). It also allows him to avoid entering into patron-client relationships with the community's small group of imperial or provincial elites (1:11; 16:17–18; Rom 16:1–2, 23).[4] Their desire to entangle him in such a web of benefits and responsibilities provides another example where cross-cutting aspects of their Roman social identity were creating problems for their in Christ identity salience (1:12). It is not that patronage was in itself sinful, but only that prioritizing those rights and responsibilities would hinder Paul in his mission. The

---

4. Briones, *Paul's Financial Policy*, 223. He takes a slightly different approach to this but is otherwise helpful.

Macedonians did not have that same misunderstanding, and thus Paul did accept financial support from them (11:22; 2 Cor 11:8–10). Gospel-informed rights and responsibilities are key identity performances in Paul's rhetorical vision of an alternative community with a distinct ethos; their group identity should be culturally relevant and therefore specific to their circumstances.

SOLUTION: MISSION AS SOCIAL IDENTIFICATION (9:19–23)

One of Paul's solutions to the problems of food offered to idols and civic engagements is mission as social identification. Paul writes in 9:19 that he is "free with respect to all"; however, he has also "made" himself "a slave to all." He acts in this way to "win more of them." Too often, this verse is read to suggest that Paul thinks he is free from Torah observance, but the freedom in view here is, on the one hand, from becoming indebted to human masters and, on the other hand, from prioritizing his own safety or advantage in his interactions with others. This freedom in turn allows him to serve others as their apostle, as one who willingly gives up certain rights for his mission among the nations.

Paul then in 9:20–21 addresses his continuing social identification with those who are part of his ethnic group: "To the Jews I became as a Jew, to win Jews." The presence of "as" suggests to many interpreters that Paul had ceased to be a Jew, or that he only identified himself as such in certain missional situations. However, it is more likely that this refers to Paul's variety of practices as he relates to Diaspora ethnic Jews generally, especially in the areas of hospitality and table fellowship, which is part of the larger context of 8:1—11:1. Paul then describes another group, "those under the law." If this simply referred to the Jews, it would be

"Do Everything for the Glory of God" (8:1—11:1)

redundant, so Paul probably had something else in view. It is quite likely that "under the law" refers to a subgroup identity, a group following a stricter halakah possibly associated with the Pharisees.[5] Paul's past as a Pharisee (Phil 3:5) would allow him to follow Pharisaic halakah to reach this group with the gospel, even though he is "not under the law" (meaning the strict halakot of this group).

The next group Paul brings up is "those outside the law." This reference to gentiles emphasizes their sinfulness (9:21; Gal 2:15). In discussing his approach to this group, Paul notes that he is "not free from God's law but" is "under Christ's law." In light of 7:17–20 where there is a calling in Christ for Jews to live as Jews, one might expect that Paul would follow his own "rule" (7:17). Yet the phrase "Christ's law" has vexed interpreters. David Rudolph suggests that it "*refers to God's law (the law of Moses) in the hand of Christ as reflected in Christ's association with sinners.*"[6] This interpretation fits well with Paul's hope to "win (*kerdanō*) those outside the law." This word is used five times in this section (9:19, 20 two times, 21, 22) suggesting that the crucial context here is mission. The Pharisees, in fact, used this term for "recruiting new members through table-fellowship and living among the masses."[7] This interpretation becomes even more likely when one considers Matt 23:15 and its description of a Pharisaic mission together with Paul's personal history claimed in Phil 3:8.

Paul's mission as social identification is further described in 9:22–23 when he writes, "to the weak I became weak, so that I might win the weak." The term "weak" is often thought to refer to those who are not in Christ. This would make sense in light of 9:23 where Paul says he does

5. Tucker, *Remain in Your Calling*, 104.
6. Rudolph, *A Jew to the Jews*, 165, italics original; Gal 6:2.
7. Ibid., 166.

all of this "for the sake of the gospel." However, Paul's work of identity construal is broader than a one-time experience (1:18; Phil 2:12). In the present context the "weak" refer to a subgroup identity within the Christ-movement in Corinth for whom eating food offered to idols had "become a stumbling block" (8:7, 9). If the earlier discussion concerning "win" is considered, especially in light of Matt 18:15, then broader aspects of identity formation are part of Paul's "gospel" mission. This subgroup may also be those who were poor and disadvantaged, and therefore more impacted by eating restrictions. They could easily have been termed "weak" in light of Roman cultural expectations of strength (1:26–29). Paul socially identifies with this group by working "with his own hands" as a "tentmaker" in Corinth and by refusing to participate in Roman patronage (4:10, 12; Acts 18:3, 11, 18). It is likely that social identification with others is part of the imitation that Paul had in mind as he instructs the Corinthians to follow him as he follows Christ (11:1; 2 Cor 6:10; 8:9; Luke 4:13–14, 21).

SOLUTION: NON-AGONISTIC SELF-DISCIPLINE (9:24–27)

Food offered to idols and civic engagements were contributing to the lack of identity salience among the Corinthians. Paul, as a bicultural mediator, draws on one distinct cultural script to highlight his desired alternative identity performance.[8] The group norms reflected in the Corinthians' language about the Isthmian games gives insight into their ethical assumptions.[9] These games reinforced the prevailing agonistic (in other words, competitive) culture which in turn supported the continued domination by the emperor,

---

8. Ehrensperger, *Paul and the Crossroads of Cultures*, 131–37.
9. Malcolm, *The World of 1 Corinthians*, 96–98.

"Do Everything for the Glory of God" (8:1—11:1)

the senate, and the provincial elites who organized them. For Paul, mutuality and relationality are the key alternatives to the competitive nature of the local expressions of imperial ideology. However, he does not want the Corinthian Christ-followers to focus so much on their ingroup relations that they become an inward-focused sect. They, therefore, need to continue to interact in the agonistic Roman colony, but this identity needs some slight correction. He begins with the imagery of a "race" and reminds the Corinthians that simply entering the "race" is not enough; one must compete "in such a way" as to "win it" (9:24). While racing imagery was used frequently in antiquity, Paul focuses on the "self-control" needed to win "an imperishable" prize, likely salvation (1 Thess 2:19; Phil 4:1; Plutarch, *Table Talk*, 5.3). He mentions the focus and discipline needed by athletes to achieve their goal (9:26). Similarly, Paul will "punish" and "enslave" his "body" so that after "proclaiming" the gospel "to others" he will "not be disqualified" himself (9:27). This reinforces the possibility of one's works being burned in the fire of judgment, mentioned earlier in the letter (3:10–15).

These verses give insight into Paul's model of conversion. It can include radical reversals as well as the gradual transformation of one's bodily practices, one's habitus.[10] Thus, identity formation is part of conversion for those in Christ. Paul can view it as a sudden past event (14:23–24; Gal 4:8–9), but also as a gradual transformation, a mold to be pressed into, and something that moves forward and backward (3:1; 9:27; 2 Cor 3:18; Phil 3:12). Thus, Paul warns the Corinthians against complacency in the formation of an in Christ social identity, especially as it relates to incorporating existing cultural scripts. Self-discipline is needed but not the present-oriented competitive drive that disregards the needs and concerns of others (11:33; 12:25).

10. Coppins, "To Eat or Not to Eat Meat?," 85–87.

PROBLEM: IDOLATRY (10:1–13)

Paul acts as a skilled manager of social identity when he states, "I do not want you to be unaware, brothers and sisters." He is building on the cognitive components of their group identity to address the potential dangers of falling into idolatry. He offers an example from Israel's history, adjusted specifically for the Corinthian Christ-followers: "our ancestors were all under the cloud" (10:1). Interpreters often see this use of "our" as the inscription of Israel's identity onto these in Christ gentiles, who then have supposedly become Israelites. However, it is unlikely that Paul sees such an end to Israel's identity. In 1:22–24, he does not confuse Jewish and gentile identity. In 7:17–24, he laid out his rule about calling in circumcision and uncircumcision. Later in 12:13, he will use the Jew and Greek pairing to show the way ethnicities continue to be relevant in Christ. This overall theologizing concerning the Christ-movement in which Jews remain Jews and gentiles remain gentiles should not disappear in the interpretation of 10:1. The phrase "our ancestors" instead indicates that gentile Christ-followers are grafted into God's family while at the same time remaining distinct from the natural branches (Rom 11:24, 25–27).

Paul uses the story of Israel's desert experience because it warns the Corinthians that even those who have been called by God can fall into immorality and idolatry. In 10:3–4, Paul alludes to Exod 16:1–36 and describes the manna the Israelites ate. Exod 17:1–7 and Num 20:2–13 refer to the water that flowed from the rock. He reminds the Corinthians that God's presence was with the Israelites then, and he connects the Israelites' experience with that of the Christ-followers by stating, "and the rock was Christ" (10:5). Then Paul makes his point: "nevertheless, God was not pleased with most of them." He thus highlights the potential limits

"Do Everything for the Glory of God" (8:1—11:1)

to God's protection. He specifically applies this new identity narrative to his audience in 10:6: "these things occurred as examples for us." By connecting them with the story of Israel, Paul provides a foundation for the ethical choices and the transformation of the Corinthians' existing identities as they relate to not desiring "evil." In 10:7, he uses ingroup and outgroup language to establish communal boundaries and to encourage the Corinthians "not" to "become idolaters as some of" the Israelites "did." He drives the point home with another story from Israel's past, the golden calf incident in Exod 32:6, to remind the Corinthians that continuing the practice of eating and drinking in the presence of an idol would eventually incur God's displeasure.

Continuing to draw from Israel's past in 10:8, Paul writes: "we must not indulge in sexual immorality," referring to Num 25:1–9 and its recording of "twenty-three thousand" who died "in a single day." Paul then encourages the Corinthians to "not put Christ to the test." He is alluding to Num 21:5–9 which describes the way "serpents" killed those who acted against God, especially in their eating and drinking. Next he highlights Num 16:41–50 where complaining about food and drink led to destruction. Paul brings his chain of Scripture references to a close in 10:11 by restating what he had said earlier: "these things happened to them to serve as an example." Further, "they were written down to instruct us." He did not chain these episodes together to shame the Christ-followers but to teach them. He puts the in Christ identity that he has been inscribing in an apocalyptic eschatological framework crafted for the time and place in which these gentiles "on whom the ends of the ages have come" find themselves. Paul's alternative communities were apocalyptic ones. Eating and drinking in the Christ-movement was not to be like eating and drinking in the rest of the empire. In 10:12, Paul writes, "so," highlighting the inference he wishes the Corinthians to take away from his argument: be careful lest you fall like those from the story of Israel. Here again, as in 4:14, he does not scold them, but encourages. He assures them that with each "testing God is faithful" and "will also provide" a means by which a person can "endure it." In this passage (10:1–13), then, Paul writes a new identity narrative for the Corinthians through the scriptural story of Israel and lets them know that the aspects of their existing identities related to immorality and idolatry must discontinue. As mentioned earlier, gentile identity in Christ continues except in areas related to immorality, idolatry, unscriptural thought patterns (2:10–16), and cultural boasting. This passage provides abundant evidence for the need for an identity transformation in Christ.

GENTILES IN CHRIST FORMED THROUGH ISRAEL'S EXAMPLE AND STORY (10:14–22)

Picking up from his earlier argument in 8:1–13, Paul extends the discussion in 10:14–22 by pointing out that even though they are correct that idols do not exist, they still cannot participate in pagan temple meals. What the Corinthians are doing is not idolatry *per se*, but it is still partnering "with demons" and so must be ruled out for those who "partake of the table of the Lord." Thus, while 10:14–22 argues differently than 8:1–13, Paul's concern is still the same; he wants to protect the identity of the community as the body of Christ and maintain holiness, and holy practices, as primary indexes of its identity.[11]

In 10:14, Paul begins with an inferential "therefore" to indicate that what follows builds on his previous assertion that the Corinthians must learn from the example of Israel. He calls the community, "my beloved," an ingroup

11. Ehrensperger, *Paul and the Crossroads of Cultures*, 196.

"Do Everything for the Glory of God" (8:1—11:1)

descriptor he had used earlier to define their social identity (4:14; see also 15:58; 2 Cor 7:1; 12:19). He then makes his identity maintenance clear: "flee from the worship of idols." Roman social identity was deeply connected with veneration of various deities, and the Corinthians needed significant guidance because separating from the broader culture while remaining integrated enough for mission often proves challenging (5:9-10). Paul then writes, "I speak as to sensible people." This comment seems to be ironic based on the earlier discussion about the need to be foolish (4:10). Similarly, Paul's call to "judge" what he says likely connects back to 6:1-11 where their inability to judge indicated a failure of their identity performance in relation to some aspect of their before Christ identity, such as sexual and economic practices. In 10:16-17, the corporate identity of the Corinthians serves as a key metaphor; the group is "one body." Paul raises two questions related to the practice of the communal meal which are designed to emphasize his main focus: the transformed nature of the community that participates in the body and blood of Christ.

In 10:18, Paul connects his current argument with what he wrote in 10:1-13, "consider the people of Israel." He reminds the Corinthians that their current experience is not too dissimilar from that of the Israelites during the Exodus, especially with regard to "altars" (Lev 7:6, 15; Deut 18:1-4). Paul incorporates participationist language throughout this section (e.g., "sharing" and "partners" in 10:16, 18 and "partake" in 10:17, 21) to emphasize the impact ethical choices have on social identity (10:20, 30). He has raised the question about the nature of the "idols" or "food sacrificed" to them (10:19). He says that the "pagans" are actually offering a "sacrifice to demons" (10:20). Therefore, Paul does not want Christ-followers to participate in eating idol meat or idolatry because these are not neutral social constructs but practices that are in conflict with their transformed identity in Christ (2 Cor 5:17). In 10:21, Paul sets forth two incompatible partnerships: that with "the Lord" and that with "demons." This shows the symbolic boundaries between Corinthian and in Christ identities, and the way they were shifting. Some areas, such as this one, required significant resocialization. Paul concludes this section with two rhetorical questions: "Or are we provoking the Lord to jealously? Are we stronger than he?" These restate the claims central to his argument. The first relates back to God's jealousy over idolatrous practices (Exod 20:5; Deut 4:24) while the second implicitly reminds the Corinthian Christ-followers of their weakness (cf. 4:10; 9:22, for example). Paul has thus completed his reflection on the impact that the Exodus tradition might have on the formation of gentile identity in Christ. Paul wants the Corinthians to avoid immorality and idolatry in its various forms so that they will not embody identity performances that do not glorify God.

SOLUTION: MIMESIS AND EMBODIMENT FOR GOD'S GLORY (10:23—11:1)

Earlier, in 8:1–13 and 10:14–22, Paul had shown that participating in pagan temple meals is not acceptable for those who follow Christ. Now he addresses further identity performances that would occur on a regular basis in relation to food and idolatry. Some interpreters think that his instructions here contradict his guidance in the earlier passages, but that is not the case. Paul begins by quoting a Corinthian slogan: "All things are lawful" (10:23). "Are lawful" (*exestin*) is better translated "are permissible." Paul is not claiming to be free from the law. Instead, he connects the Corinthians' slogan to Psalm 24:1, "the earth and its fullness are the

"Do Everything for the Glory of God" (8:1—11:1)

Lord's" (10:26), despite the claims of pagan creation narratives. Nothing is inherently unclean, either, which would have been Paul's previous evaluation of pagans from the perspective of Judaism. For Paul, much of gentile culture is good and might be enjoyed by Christ-followers. Further, the "liberty" referred to in 10:29, rather than being a claim of universal freedom from the law, refers to freedom for the gentiles from their past bondage to idols.

Paul is addressing those uncertain situations in which Christ-followers would come into contact with food that might have been offered to idols.[12] Paul's halakic stance is not to question the food's provenance. Further, the seller of the meat or the pagan host must be taken into consideration. The nature of the food, which Paul has already declared is part of God's good creation (10:25, 28), is not the most important factor, and pagan rituals do not change its nature. Therefore, food of unknown origin may be eaten in non-ritual settings as long as one "partakes" of it "with thankfulness" (10:30). However, if the seller of the meat or the pagan host or someone else points out that the same food has been part of a ritual, it cannot be eaten by the Christ-follower (10:28). Paul's argument here is the same as in the earlier passages. To be seen by others (a weaker sibling in Christ, a shop owner, or a host) as participating in that which is explicitly associated with a pagan deity constitutes sin for those following Christ.

Gentiles in Christ cannot participate in these practices, whether in civic settings or private contexts, because to do so jeopardizes the holiness and identity salience of the group (8:9–10; 10:20, 27–29). Paul's goal is exclusive loyalty to the God of Israel for these in Christ gentiles, and it is on this basis that he invents gentile Christ-following social identity. He summarizes it this way: "So, whether you eat or

12. Tomson, *Paul and the Jewish Law*, 208.

drink, or whatever you do, do everything for the glory of God" (10:31). What is an acceptable identity performance from Paul's point of view? Anything that can be done to God's glory. This means that an in Christ social identity is open but has limitations such as "give no offence" (10:32) and "not seeking" one's "own advantage" (10:33). Such limitations function as gospel-oriented boundaries for the community; ethical embodiment is practiced "so that they," non-Christ-followers, "may be saved." This aptly describes mission as social identification (see earlier 5:9–10).

Paul offers himself as a model to be followed: "Be imitators of me, as I am of Christ" (11:1; see also 4:16). Leadership is a type of social influence where a person is viewed by the group to be more prototypical and influential than others in a particular setting.[13] In this form of leadership, the leader represents the group and leads via mimesis (imitation/representation). Paul is not calling the Corinthians to follow him exactly since he was a Jewish Christ-follower and gentiles should not imitate him in every particular. Rather, he wants them to follow his and Christ's example of serving, being humble, and obeying biblical commands.[14]

DISCUSSION QUESTIONS

1. When it comes to food offered to idols, Paul thinks the Corinthians are correct in terms of their knowledge but not in terms of their relationships towards others. What would that mean for you in terms of self-imposed restrictions on certain cultural practices?

---

13. Starling, *UnCorinthian Leadership*, 10. He takes a slightly different approach to defining leadership but aligns quite closely with the approach to Paul's practice argued for here.

14. Ehrensperger, *Paul and The Dynamics of Power*, 137–54.

"Do Everything for the Glory of God" (8:1—11:1)

How would you keep a Christian with a weak conscience from dominating the social practices of a faith community?

2. This chapter demonstrated that Paul continued to be Torah observant in his mission to the nations. How does that align with your understanding of Paul's law-free gospel? Do you think that Israel's covenantal identity continues now that Christ has come? Do you think that Paul would follow his own rule from 7:17–24 to remain in his calling and not to seek to undo his circumcision (as a Jewish male)?

3. Paul was presented as a bicultural mediator, as a go-between. In what way could you begin to practice mediating between a gospel-defined culture and the culture found in the broader society? Paul sought to transform the competitive nature of the Roman world. What is a similar cultural ordering principle today and how might you engage it for the sake of mission, and transform it within the church?

4. Paul reads Israel's Scriptures in a way that differs from the normal historical-grammatical approach; he sees Christ as the interpretive key (10:5). Can we engage in a similar interpretive approach? What would be some suggested guidelines for this practice to avoid subjectivity in interpretation?

5. Paul's overarching principle for embodying an in-Christ identity is to do everything for the glory of God. What would it mean to you personally and to your ministry context if this became a salient principle? Are there any restrictions on the application of this principle? If so, isn't that imposing on another person's liberty in Christ? How might mimesis (imitation) help with this social conflict?

8

"ALL THINGS SHOULD BE DONE DECENTLY AND IN ORDER" (11:2—14:40)

INTRODUCTION

MANY HEAR PAUL'S INSTRUCTIONS concerning decency and order as an idea that is past its sell date, a spoiled container of universal authoritarian discourse that has contributed to societal ills throughout church history. The naturalization of male and female roles is nothing new, but Paul's teaching in this section of the letter is not the same as what one would have found in the nineteenth-century publication, *The Englishwoman's Domestic Magazine*. Rather, in these chapters Paul addresses the way gender identities and the meal table are transformed within the Christ-movement, the way unity amid diversity reveals one's membership in Christ's body, and the way love constructs a doxological social identity. Such an identity is one that opens itself to God through the regular practice of praise, to allow his continued work to transform their identity not only towards holiness, but also towards the cultures around them to invite more people to become part of their practice of praise. Readers, as they work through these challenging chapters, should recognize the rhetorical nature of these texts since they were written to address specific situations and framed to persuade the original audience. They should also remember that when readers study Paul and make claims about topics such as leadership and gender they are at the same time studying and making claims about themselves.

THE CONTINUATION OF GENDER HIERARCHIES (11:2–16)

After addressing identity and ethical issues in the first part of the letter, in 11:2—16:12, Paul addresses further issues related to the group's ethos. His rhetorical vision is that the Corinthian Christ-followers are to be an alternative community with an ethos distinct from that of the Roman culture in Corinth. To facilitate this, Paul, as a manager of identity in competition with other identity managers in the social world of the Corinthian Christ-followers, needs to empower and mobilize the group members to solve their collective problems and to attain their collective goal of embodying the gospel message within the gentile Christ-movement. He uses processes similar to those that social identity theorists have discovered effectively turn "you" and "me" into "us." Paul's identity-forming work addresses gender issues, meal practices, spiritual gifts, unity amid diversity, love, doxological practices, group beliefs, and the group's future involvement in the gentile mission. This chapter of the book highlights briefly those aspects of the letter that might be clarified by reading it through the lens of social identity theory.

The way in which gender identities continued within the Christ-movement contributed to social disorder during the worship gatherings. Paul first "commends" the Corinthians because they "remember" Paul and "maintain the traditions" that had been previously passed on (11:2). The concept of group prototypicality is an important part of Paul's approach to identity formation. He often includes a memory component when discussing group prototypes (e.g., Timothy in 4:17; Paul in 11:1–2; and Stephanas in 1:16; 16:15–17). Collective memory is a crucial process for the development of exemplary figures and provides flexibility in the application of the halakic "traditions" they had received. After describing a series of relationships, Paul focuses specifically on the way a person "who prays or prophesies" does so in relation to continuing gender identities (11:3–5). In Paul's cultural context, a woman should pray or prophesy while wearing a "veil," while a man should not "have his head veiled" (11:6–7). Men engaged in Roman imperial religious practices pulled their outer garment forward over their head while sacrificing. Thus, Paul may again be addressing confusion on the part of some in the assembly about the transformation of existing identities. Associations with idolatry should not continue within the Christ-movement.[1] About women, the situation is more unclear although public veiling was expected and regulated by law. It communicated honor and provided protection for women. The problem likely emerged when the assembly

---

1. Peppiatt, *Women and Worship at Corinth*, 81–82, offers a slightly different understanding of the problems associated with masculine identity practices.

"All Things Should Be Done Decently and in Order" (11:2—14:40)

met in private or household space since in such a close kinship setting a veil might not be worn.[2]

Paul, in 11:7-10, enculturates these gentiles in Christ into Israel's symbolic universe through his reasoning with Scripture. Here he describes "man" as one made in "the image and reflection of God" while a "woman is the reflection of man" (11:7). He offers a combined reading of Gen 1:26-27 and 2:21-23 with a possible allusion to Ps 8:5-8 that focuses on the sequence of creation (11:8-9). (The NIV translates Ps 8:5 in a way that, unlike the NRSV, helps readers see this possible allusion, and shows a possible reason for Paul's reference to "angels" in 11:10.) Paul's statement, however, does not establish secondary status as part of the nature of women since both genders are made in the image of God (Gen 1:27; 5:1-2). From the Genesis account, Paul concludes that "a woman ought to have a symbol of authority on her head" (11:10). The NRSV marginal reading notes that "a symbol" is not in the Greek. Thus, Paul could be understood to mean that women should have the authority to decide whether to wear a veil or to do their hair in unconventional ways (cf. Rom 14:5 on another issue), possibly to equalize status among various classes of women. However, while there is a certain amount of halakic flexibility in Paul's instruction, the context of 11:2-16 suggests that he prefers a social behavior more in line with traditional Roman expectations. This may be another example of mission as social identification: Identify closely enough with the culture so that a gospel identity may be embodied in the presence of those who have not yet come to follow Christ (5:9-10; 10:31—11:1).

The transformation of existing gender identities and hierarchies is hinted at in 11:11-12 when Paul writes "in the Lord woman is not independent of man." This suggests

2. Westfall, *Paul and Gender*, 31, 33-34.

that Paul's halakah has been informed by the group's shared life in Christ. Interdependence and mutuality between the genders is made explicit when he writes "nor man independent of woman." These two verses work against appeals to the earlier verses (11:8–9) to suggest that Paul thinks that women are somehow subordinate to men—Paul is not a hierarchalist when it comes to gender identities. He continues, "woman came from man ... man comes through woman," as he appeals to the common Jewish idea of creation and the ongoing role that women play in the household structure (Job 14:1; *1 Esdras* 4:15–17). From Paul's Jewish perspective, the Roman household structure is not inviolable since for Paul, "all things come from God" (3:21–23; 8:6; 10:26; 11:3). Some of the confusion about gender behavior in communal gatherings that Paul addresses in this section (and about eating practices in the next) occurred because the groups were meeting in Roman household space, and proper behavior within the home clashed with proper behavior for worship in sacred (read as *ekklēsia*) space.[3] For Paul, gender differences continue but mutuality and relationality are to characterize the group's identity performances since all ultimately belong to God.

In 11:13–16, Paul concludes his argument by asking the Corinthians to "judge for yourselves" concerning the appropriate way for "a woman to pray." He then relies on an argument from "nature" and appeals to the social discourse of honor and shame (11:14–15). After this he ends his advice on this topic by pointing out "if anyone is disposed to be contentious—we have no such customs, nor do the churches of God." Why would Paul insert a reference to other churches here? Is it to exert rhetorical leverage and cajole the Corinthians into submission, as is often thought? He is clearly setting boundaries for who is part of the ingroup

---

3. Tucker, *Remain in Your Calling*, 159–85.

and who is not. Also, his appeal to existing "customs" does legitimate his authority to direct the community. However, such an interpretation should be moderated by the way hierarchy and power in Paul's social formation are nuanced and relational. His approach has its basis in the Jewish concept of mimesis as a pattern of life to be followed rather than in a domineering power-over approach to leadership (see discussion at 4:17; 11:1). Paul is better understood to be negotiating the Christ-followers' social identity through his initial commendation of them (11:2), his understanding of cultural practices (11:4–6), his appeals to Israel's scriptural tradition (11:7–10), and finally through his openness to other conclusions on this issue (11:13), although he does ultimately want their behavior to line up with that of the rest of "the churches of God," the other gentile assemblies who are part of the Pauline Christ-movement (11:16). For Paul, gender identities are not obliterated in Christ; they are transformed in ways that are in both continuity and discontinuity with existing cultural scripts.

THE TRANSFORMATION OF TABLE FELLOWSHIP (11:17–34)

The way in which table fellowship had changed within the Christ-movement was also adding to the social upheaval within the community. For Paul, household space was transformed into an *ekklēsia* ritual space when the community gathered. He was not trying to obliterate Roman household practices; rather, he was creating a transformed space in which existing household structures continue to be relevant elements of *ekklēsia* space. Thus, in Paul's discussion of table fellowship, he continues to promote the ideal of unity that admits differences, rather than an ideal of conformity. Unlike Paul's approach to veils in 11:2–16,

Paul does not "commend" the Corinthians; rather, when they "come together," their identity performance reduces the salience of their in Christ social identity (11:17). Paul therefore brings up the existence of "divisions" again and uses social influence by stating, "To some extent I believe it." This heightens his identity-forming work by expressing a certain level of alterity from them. Often, interpreters argue that Paul sought to remove subgroup identifications within the community, but that is not the case. In 11:19, he recognizes that "factions," existing ingroup identities, serve a positive purpose: they reveal those who are "genuine" followers of Christ. Paul, in this letter, does not seek to erase existing senses of belonging; rather, he wants to reprioritize these under the superordinate identity, an identity in Christ that does not erase difference. (See earlier discussion on 1:12; 3:23; 7:18, 20.)

When Paul writes in 11:20 that the meal the Corinthians have been participating in is "not really . . . the Lord's supper," he is managing one expression of their social identity. Rituals such as meals should encourage ingroup belonging, but in Corinth they were producing social alienation since early arrivers were eating all the food, leaving late-comers "hungry." Even worse, some were getting "drunk" during these gatherings (11:21). Paul reminds the group that they should "eat and drink" at home before they gather and that their current practice shows "contempt for the church of God" by humiliating some within the Christ-following community (11:22).

Paul's solution is to engage the group members in a renewed set of social practices in which they experience and express their in Christ social identity. He does this first by reminding them of the tradition Paul had "received from the Lord" and previously had "handed on to" the Corinthians (11:23–26). They had apparently discontinued

"All Things Should Be Done Decently and in Order" (11:2—14:40)

the part of the communal meal referenced in the Gospel tradition in favor of a Roman *convivium* (banquet) in which aspects of imperial ideology, social hierarchy, and patronage were reinforced. Instead, Paul, like Philo, envisions that they will "wait for one another" (11:22) and all, "whoever ... eats" (11:27), will share the communal meal (Philo, *On The Contemplative Life*, 48–63, 68–69, 71–72, 85). This transformed approach to table fellowship will allow the Corinthians to avoid eating in "an unworthy manner" by taking time to "examine yourselves," "discerning the body" so that they will "not be condemned along with the world" (11:27–28). These guidelines structure social relationships and order communal life in Christ in light of the problems that had emerged based on both nested and cross-cutting identities.[4] To the new identity narrative he provides in 11:17–34, Paul adds the promise that when he comes to Corinth he "will give" them "instructions" concerning "other things" (11:34).

THE TRANSFORMATION OF EXISTING IDENTITIES AND SPIRITUAL GIFTS (12:1–11)

Along with gender and meal issues, there was a general lack of participation in the ritual life of the community by those whose "spiritual gifts" were seen as less honorable. The use of the phrase "now concerning" (*peri de*) indicates another topic that the Corinthians had asked about (8:1). The contents of this section suggests that "tongues," defined as "a gift of humanly incomprehensible speech," was their primary concern.[5] This does not, however, mean that identity concerns are absent. By bringing up the Corinthians' identity as "pagans," *ethnē* (better translated "gentiles"), Paul is not

4. Barentsen, *Emerging Leadership*, 97.
5. Barclay, *1 Corinthians*, 1127.

saying that they are no longer gentiles, but that one aspect of their existing identity, idolatry, no longer describes who they are. This rejection of idolatry does not require them to convert to Judaism; thus they become in some ways ex-pagan pagans.[6] Paul is inventing gentile identity in Christ as those from the nations are brought into the family of God. It seems that, just as with food offered to idols, some of the Corinthians were confused over this identity transformation and even misconstrued an early creedal affirmation such as "Jesus is Lord" (12:3), perhaps as a magical phrase, or as a criticism of the Roman empire. Thus, Paul's teaching concerning "spiritual gifts" was at the same time the communication of his understanding of early Christ-movement identity.

In 12:4–11, Paul wants to encourage broader participation in the ritual life of the community. He does this by encouraging the Corinthians not to make value judgments on one gift over another since "the same Spirit" gives them all, and they are designed "for the common good" (12:4, 7). So one who has been "given" the "utterance of wisdom" should not despise the one who has been given the "utterance of knowledge," because, as Paul will argue in the next section, the Christ-followers are all part of one body. Therefore, they should not think of each other as part of an outgroup (12:15–26). Even if one were to construe the body imagery Paul uses the way the Stoics did, as a unifying cosmology that renders individuals insignificant, a different kind of communal identity would emerge since individual identity practices continue in the body of Christ.

It is evident from Paul's discussion that this new community should be formed by the work of the "Spirit . . . Lord . . . God" (12:4–6). Their identity, therefore, will be

---

6. Fredriksen, "The Question of Worship," 182, was one of the first persons to frame this group in such a manner.

unique as they are empowered and gifted by God's Spirit to represent God in Corinth. From a Tajfelian perspective, Paul adds a cognitive component here (a group formed by God), an evaluative component (a new way to consider the gifts of others), and an emotional factor (all are now appreciated as gifted members for the common good of the group).[7] Finally, Paul reminds the Corinthians that these gifts and their membership in this community are the result of the Spirit's choosing, not their own, although their distinct identities and choices affect the group (cf. 12:11, 31; 14:1). The charismatic nature of the Corinthian community undoubtedly contributed to Paul's advice about leadership maintenance and identity formation as he conducted his pastoral ministry from afar.

THE EMERGENCE OF UNITY AMID DIVERSITY IN THE SPIRIT (12:12–31)

The unity of the body in the midst of diversity is the primary point Paul's "body" and limbs imagery makes (12:12–13). This is reinforced by the baptismal tradition cited in 12:13, although, unlike in Gal 3:28, here the male and female categories are not included. Paul only mentions "Jews or Greeks, slaves or free." Baptism, for Paul, is an identity performance that transfers one into the body of Christ and is the embodiment of a transformed identity (2 Cor 5:17). This transformed identity does not remove existing identities, such as Jew, Greek, slave and free, since Paul continues to recognize that such categories exist (12:13). Ethnic and social identities do not affect salvation; however, they do continue to be important in Christ, as long as they are deprioritized (7:17–24). The Corinthians had misunderstood (3:3–4). Many saw a continuation of existing identities

7. Tajfel, "Interindividual Behaviour," 28.

without any need for change. For Paul, these identities were not to be opposed completely but transformed in areas relating to immorality, idolatry, unscriptural thought patterns, and cultural boasting.

As highlighted in Chapters 1 and 3, honor and shame were key ordering principles in the Roman empire. In 12:14–26, Paul uses them again, this time to illustrate that a properly functioning body is diverse (12:14). He structures the first part of his illustration (12:15–16) from the perspective of the marginalized, those to whom others say, "You don't belong." However, he also has another group in view: those who are prioritizing other identities, and therefore, in some identity performances, saying to themselves, "Well, I don't really belong to the followers of Christ." Paul argues for an increase in "honor" for those who might otherwise feel shame based either on the evaluation of others or of themselves (12:23–25). For Paul, "Christ" is the head of one "body," a body in which unity allows for diversity among those who are "individually members of it" (12:12–13, 25, 27).

In 12:27–31, Paul's discussion of "the body of Christ" illustrates unity amid diversity in the Spirit and is not simply theological. Since it occurs in the context of debates over leadership, it seems evident that the leadership subgroup that Paul left in Corinth had not been able to reinforce an in-Christ social identity among the Corinthians. The listing of spiritual gifts in this chapter includes "apostles, prophets, and teachers," all of whom were "appointed in the church" by "God" (12:28). It is too early a stage in the development of the Christ-movement to conclude that it indicates a hierarchy of titles or positions. It is more likely that these were functions based on individual gifting.[8] Two gifts in particular are important for the present discussion of leadership:

8. Tucker, "Religious Leaders," 181–84.

"forms of assistance" and "forms of leadership." While these might possibly represent early forms of what later became deacons and elders, the plurals do suggest that there were different opinions about the nature and function of leadership. Various leaders within the Christ-movement were discussed elsewhere in this book (see 1:1, 14–15; 16:15–17; Rom 16:1, 23). If some of the debates going on within the community centered on different approaches to leadership, "Stephanas" and those associated with his "household" seem to be the ones that embody Paul's vision for communal life since he instructs the Corinthians to follow them as managers of their social identity (16:16).

AN ETHOS OF LOVE: A GOSPEL IDENTITY MADE SALIENT (13:1-13)

A group's ethos is built up of individual ethical choices and practices which emerge from the prior identity narrative that has been absorbed. In Chapter 13, Paul continues to restructure the activities within the community that are causing problems, likely because of both nested and crosscutting identities. Yet the in-Christ identity has only come into existence as a result of God's acts of love: the gospel itself and God's love that has been poured out through the Spirit (6:11; Rom 5:5). So, love has become a defining characteristic of this alternative community which should then reflect a distinct ethos that contrasts with the broader civic community (8:1–13; 13:1—14:1; 16:14).

Correct ritual performance is not the goal; that was what Roman imperial practices emphasized. For them only the right performance could ensure that the rite "worked" in the sense of engaging the help of the gods. Paul is more concerned with promoting "love" as one of the group's norms (13:1–4, 13). Group members ought to embody "love" by committing themselves to the norms of the broader Christ-movement, in which faith is more of a relational concept than a cognitive one (2:5; 13:13; 15:14, 17). One could "speak in tongues, have prophetic powers, knowledge, give away possessions," and even be willing to be martyred, but these are comparatively "nothing" without "love." Paul is not saying that the Corinthians ought not to engage in those actions since most of these fit into the category of "gifts" given by the Spirit (12:8–10). However, he is deprioritizing them under the superordinate value of love. He then makes his vision for the group's ethos more concrete through a cognitive representation of the behavior that that love produces: "love is patient, kind, not envious, not boastful, not arrogant or rude, and does not rejoice in wrongdoing," etc. (13:4–7). As the list continues it becomes evident that the aspects of love he highlights relate directly to the identity-based problems evident throughout the letter. (See, for example, the correspondences between 13:4 and 3:3, 21; 13:5 and 6:7; 8:1; and 13:6 and 5:2.)

As mentioned earlier, one of the problems with some of the Corinthians was an over-identification with Roman imperial eschatology and its pretentious claim to an empire without end (Virgil, *Aeneid*, 1.278). For Paul, on the contrary, it is "love" that "never ends" (13:8). His apocalyptic perspective informs his argument in 13:8–13, as it did in 4:8. He makes clear that even some of the ritual practices that form an in-Christ identity are temporary and thus need to be re-categorized socially (13:8–10). The Corinthians had apparently not been given the right categories to allow them to distinguish between important ethical practices (such as love) and less important functions and gifts (such as tongues). Paul negotiates with them what he thinks is prototypical and normative. Paul describes the transformation of identity that he is working to promote using the image of a "child" transforming into an "adult." It is adult behavior that a mature Christ-follower embodies and "knows" (13:11–12). Paul concludes his discussion of the group's gospel-defined ethos characterized by love by offering an alternative to both the Aristotelian and Stoic virtues such as self-restraint and freedom: "now faith, hope, and love abide, these three; and the greatest of these is love."[9]

DOXOLOGICAL IDENTITY: AN OTHERS-ORIENTED COMMUNAL PRACTICE (14:1–12)

A doxological social identity emerges from an awareness of one's membership in a group that embodies specific ritual practices that reinforce maximal distinctiveness over time. In Chapter 13 Paul reinforced this identity in contrast to Roman glory and virtue (see also Rom 15:7–13). He continues to offer a vision for the community that worships together in a way that remains aware of other worshippers, reinforcing unity amid their continuing diversity (7:20; 12:13). He gives the Corinthians a path to follow: "pursue love." This admonition is the application of his speech in praise of love. He follows up with a reference to "spiritual gifts," bringing the topic back to his earlier concern (12:1; 13:1–13). His point in 14:1–40 is that to "prophesy" is the most important gift because it forms the communal ethos; it is "building up the church" in ways other gifts do not (14:12).

Paul does not want to downplay the ongoing practice of "those who speak in a tongue" since he identifies himself as one of them (14:6, 11, 18). He is one of them in this embodied practice but also in the formation process he wants them to imitate. Paul's concern is that "to prophesy," which is more communal in nature, is being neglected in

9. Esler, *Conflict and Identity*, 322.

favor of "tongues," which is more individualistic (14:5). Prophesying would result in "the building up of the church" (14:12), and the subgroups aligning their ritual practices with Paul's rhetorical vision would be differentiated from the others ("foreigner"; 14:11). This others-orientation for the purpose of transformation is not just an internal ordering principle, it has an outward mission focus to it as well.

DOXOLOGICAL IDENTITY: OUTWARD-ORIENTED MISSION PRACTICE (14:13–25)

Paul is not discrediting the "one who speaks in a tongue." He simply wants all spiritual speech to keep mission to others in mind (14:13). He is not trying to form a closed community, but one whose ritual life is mission-focused. So, when ecstatic speech was practiced, it needed to be in such a way that, when "outsiders or unbelievers" came in, they would not question whether members of the community were "out of your mind" (14:23). In this mission as social identification, existing identities continue to matter to facilitate such mission (7:17; 9:20–21). Paul again uses himself as the ingroup prototype for the community since he practices both types of speech, one or the other depending on the context (15:14–15, 18–19). He is reminding them that the proper use of "spiritual gifts" gives them the cognitive, evaluative, and emotional resources necessary to properly construct a doxological social identity that will stabilize the community and reinforce the Pauline mission in Corinth (1:12, 26; 2:16; 5:9–10; 6:6; 7:17–24; 10:27–28; 14:23).

"All Things Should Be Done Decently and in Order" (11:2—14:40)

DOXOLOGICAL IDENTITY: LIMITS AND RESTRICTIONS ON COMMUNAL PRACTICES (14:26–40)

The maximal distinctiveness from the civic community that Paul seeks to inscribe among the Christ-followers has certain limitations. He answers his question, "What should be done?" (14:26), with his overarching social ordering principle: "all things should be done decently and in order" (14:40). Public decorum was important to Roman social life, so again Paul builds on and transforms aspects of local identity. As in a Jewish voluntary association, Paul provides rules or halakah for communal life, "when you come together" (14:26). The need for such rules suggests the existence of subgroups that gathered together as one larger group at various times (11:17; Rom 16:23). Paul provides rules, a form of identity management, for the practice of prophecy and "tongues" in such larger gatherings (14:27–31). However, Paul is thinking beyond the local level, as can be seen in his reference to "all the churches of the saints" (14:33b; cf. 11:16). Paul's identity management in this section asks the Corinthians to adjust themselves to his norms because they are part of a larger network of Christ-followers around the eastern Mediterranean basin.

Paul's gender-based restrictions in 14:34–35 on speaking in the community seem confusing to the reader in light of his earlier rule in 11:2–16 which provided guidelines for women's full participation in the ritual life of the community. While the debates over this passages cannot be solved here, in the broader context of 14:26–40 Paul is narrowly addressing disorder within the larger communal gatherings and the way each member should contribute to the building up of others in these communal settings. His restrictions, therefore, are group-based (14:28, 30, 35). Even the practice of "prophets" is similarly restricted (14:32, 35). If one keeps in mind that this letter addresses a specific problem in a specific context, one can conclude that a culturally defined identity performance was creating a problem similar to the one addressed in 11:2–16. The passages do not contradict one another; there are likely two different types of speech occurring, and one is regulated differently than the other (11:5; 14:34–35). So, the silence (14:34) relates narrowly to the specific instance of disruption. It may be that wives were publically evaluating the prophecy of their husbands (14:29), and Paul argues that this contradicts "the law" and the created order, which Paul does not want to overturn (11:8–9; 14:34). For Paul, the formation of a doxological social identity may involve limitations on one's identity performance especially in those situations where its performance might interfere with ingroup identity salience (10:23).

DISCUSSION QUESTIONS

1. Paul offers advice for the ways existing gender identities are transformed within the Christ-movement. How should we, or should we apply those teachings today? How does his teaching on love impact the way we think about secondary gender identities? Can you think of other secondary gender identities? If so, how would we apply Paul's instructions for those individuals?

2. Should participation in the Lord's Supper be primarily a communal or an individualistic experience? Why does it tend to be individualistic? There have been church history debates concerning the frequency of the Eucharist. Does thinking about the communal meal as ritualized mission help? Does thinking about

"All Things Should Be Done Decently and in Order" (11:2—14:40)

ritual in identity-forming ways help you think about the necessity of worship habits that embody being in Christ?

3. How can Paul's imagery of the body of Christ help us form diverse faith communities? What are some of the challenges of living closely with people that remain different?

4. Ecstatic speech was divisive in the first century in Corinth, and it remains controversial in some settings today. How can Paul's approach to the issue help you talk about tongues and prophecy with those who differ from you?

5. Paul was clearly concerned with issues of order. Why? Church practices and structures are contact zones of identity formation. How can the principle of order be misused? What would a transformative approach to power look like in relation to church conflict?

9

"LET ALL YOU DO BE DONE IN LOVE" (15:1—16:24)

INTRODUCTION

IN 1942, THE WHITE Rose Society, a German student movement, began to oppose the atrocities being committed by Hitler and members of the Nazi Party. They felt compelled to do so by their understanding of their identity as both Christians and Germans. The lives of Hans and Sophie Scholl and the others ended in death as their leaflet distribution scheme was eventually uncovered, although now they are celebrated in Germany as heroes for standing up against the evil of their day. Such a whole-hearted outworking of one's identities is one example of the type of behavior Paul is encouraging in this last section of 1 Corinthians. He brings the letter to a close by emphasizing the practical

"Let All You Do Be Done in Love" (15:1—16:24)

ways that a gospel identity informs life, so that all is done in love. He challenges prevailing views of death and the future, calls Christ-followers to economic generosity, and lays out his vision for the transformation of social identity in Christ. While readers may not be called to the same heroic action as the members of the White Rose Society, the same call for doing justice to those inside and outside the community still remains (2 Cor 8:13–15; Mic 6:6, 8; Isa 58:6–14; Deut 24:17–18).

GOSPEL IDENTITY: BY GOD'S GRACE I AM WHAT I AM (15:1-19)

The gospel message was foundational to the proclamation of the alternative community with a distinct ethos that Paul sought to form in Corinth, along with individuals transformed by God's grace. A shared group belief in the resurrection, furthermore, was central to the earliest Christ-movement (15:4–8). However, the identity performance of some in Corinth had begun to set this aside: "how can some of you say there is no resurrection of the dead?" (15:12). Shared group beliefs are integral to identity salience. If one wants to understand the nature of a group, then one must understand the group's beliefs.[1] First Corinthians 15:12 suggests that a new identity narrative had taken hold in Corinth, one that was not in unison with the gospel discourse they had received (15:1–4). The reasons for this are unclear. It could have been an issue of cultural translation in Roman and Jewish contexts that did not have ideological room for this belief, or this identity narrative without the resurrection could have resulted from Paul's earlier focus on the cross as central (2:2).[2] Either way, the categories that

1. Bar-Tal, *Group Beliefs*, 39.
2. Ehrensperger, *Paul and the Crossroads of Cultures*, 1–13, on

governed the thinking of the Corinthian Christ-followers did not match those that Paul wanted them to develop. If the problem was that the Corinthians continued to claim participation in the Christ-following community while behaving according to Corinthian and/or Greek or Roman norms, that would explain why Paul quotes a Corinthian slogan and a Greek play (15:32–33). There seems to be confusion over the way existing identities are reprioritized in Christ (7:18; 10:31; 12:2). These cross-cutting identity dilemmas, where the Corinthians' in Christ identity intersects their civic and cultural identities, are evident throughout 1 Corinthians, but more specifically here it seems that existing social identifications were negating shared group beliefs, such as resurrection and embodiment, that were essential to the gospel tradition.[3]

Gospel identity is not only a result of shared group beliefs; it is also a result of a work of God. After describing Christ's appearance to him and his persecution of the earliest Jesus followers, Paul writes in 15:10, "by the grace of God I am what I am." He thus highlights his sense of self, of the way he differs from other Christ-followers. It is not that others have not received God's grace, but for Paul this gift of grace gives him his sense of mission and the focus for who he is and what he does. Even though this sounds like an individual identity, it is actually still an issue of group belonging. Paul is part of a network of others involved in the gentile mission (see below 16:5–12), and the context of 15:8–11 highlights the interpersonal and intergroup continuum that is crucial to social identity. Yet, although his self-categorization as an "apostle" seems to be contested, he still ends the list of witnesses with himself (9:1–3; 15:8, 9–10). It is, in fact, because of Paul's previous persecution

---

cultural translation.

3. Barentsen, *Emerging Leadership*, 83–85.

"Let All You Do Be Done in Love" (15:1—16:24)

of the movement that he has come to understand the nature of God's "grace." After this interpersonal digression, he brings other leaders and himself together in an inclusive "we," reminding them that Christ's resurrection is central to the gospel of grace, a message they "proclaim" which the Corinthians had "come to believe" (15:11).

As mentioned above, belief in the resurrection is integral to a gospel identity. So, in 15:12–19, Paul summarizes why the Corinthians should maintain this group belief. First, if the idea of the bodily "resurrection" is false then "Christ has not been raised" (15:13). Thus, if he is dead, the Corinthians' "faith is in vain" (15:14), and the authorizing discourse of the apostles would be untruthful (15:15). Second, Paul offers a slightly different argument: if Christ has not risen bodily, then "you are still in your sins" (15:16–17). So, those "in Christ" who "have died" are ultimately lost (15:18). This idea would destroy all hope, and "we," Christ-followers, would be "of all people most pitied" (15:19). With this argument, Paul is ensuring the coherence of the group. Social identity is formed through categorization of ingroups and outgroups, but that is not the only factor. Shared group beliefs provide a basis for the ongoing existence of the group. For Paul, without a belief in the resurrection of Christ and its accompanying hope in their own resurrection through God's grace, there is no reason for the Christ-groups to continue.

APOCALYPTIC IDENTITY FORMATION: THE TRANSFORMATION OF VIEWS OF DEATH (15:20–34)

In 15:20–22, Paul begins to reveal an Adam-Christ parallel that sees "Christ" as the last Adam, which addresses the issue of prototypical group leaders. This section is a good example of the way Paul combines social and theological concerns (15:20): "Christ has been raised from the dead, the first fruits of those who have died" (15:20). Paul connects the social identity of the Corinthians and their ethical behavior with the future promise of resurrection. This apocalyptic outlook is a cognitive identity-forming practice designed to get them to think differently about a core element of early Christ-movement discourse: Christ's resurrection. When Paul states that "all die in Adam" and "all will be made alive in Christ" (15:22), he is following the logic of the corporate personality, a kind of logic often missed in individualistic cultures. Paul's desire is for the Corinthians to align their behaviors with the prototype—Christ. It seems that a view had arisen that embodied behavior was secondary when it came to Christ-movement identity (6:12–20). As a result, some began to downplay the reality of their own bodily resurrection, as well as to doubt the resurrection of Christ. However, Paul is convinced that the set of beliefs associated with this social identity will motivate them to pursue self-enhancement through group allegiance and to reject their current status quo of mistaken indexes of identity.

Paul then outlines his understanding of the eschatological order (15:23–28). Christ's resurrection is the "first fruits" of the new age, which continues until the "coming" of "Christ" for "those who belong" to him (15:23). This group will be raised up and the "kingdom" given to "God the Father" after Christ has "destroyed every ruler and every authority and power" (15:24). Paul has an apocalyptic hope positioned in this time and space in which victory over death is manifest as God's kingdom takes political shape. This is likely another critique of those who rely too much on Roman imperial ideology. Caesar Augustus presented himself as the father of the country, and in Corinth one

"Let All You Do Be Done in Love" (15:1—16:24)

inscription dating to the first century describes Claudius as the "father of the fatherland." Thus, although Paul's description of God as Father does not have to be a critique of the emperor, his words at least speak to a topic that would require cultural translation in Roman Corinth. This intersection of Roman Corinthian and in Christ identities is repeated immediately by Paul's mention of Christ's "coming"; the same term could be used to announce the coming of the emperor. The combination, then, suggests that Paul is subverting Roman imperial ideology. Finally, the use of "ruler" and "authority" connects back to 2:6-9 where the Roman provincial officials were in view. Paul then is warning the Corinthians that in the end God's "kingdom" will be established, and that forming their identity primarily within the network of Roman imperial values is not a wise choice. Paul therefore offers an alternative identity forming discourse, one in which the second Adam becomes the prototype for transformation. He is bringing about a new order, although its completion must await a future realization (15:26-28; see further below 15:45-49).

In 15:29-34, Paul continues to transform the Corinthians' view of death through a series of rhetorical questions designed to clarify the social implications of the gospel about Christ's resurrection. First, 15:29 brings up another water practice that seems to be diffusing their identity, "baptism on behalf of the dead." This ritual practice was likely done for some followers of Christ who died before they had been baptized. Paul's main goal is not to criticize the ritual but to point out the futility of such a practice if the group believes that there is no resurrection. In his next effort to recategorize the Corinthian Christ-followers' thinking about death, Paul uses himself as an example of one who suffers and is close to "death" for the cause of Christ (15:30-34). It appears that the Christ-followers in Corinth had good relations with the broader civic community and thus did not experience persecution; however, Paul's point is that if there is no resurrection, then his own efforts would be a colossal waste of his life which could rather be spent seeking pleasure (Seneca, *Moral Letters to Lucilius*, 75). This description of his own life acknowledges his quite un-Roman cultural understanding of masculinity, including his exposure to death, and the power that he both has and doesn't have in this existence in between Jewish and Roman views of masculinity (15:31–32). His description would sound quite surprising to the Corinthian Christ-believers, especially when he is competing with them for the shape of the salient in Christ identity narrative, and this alteration of Roman masculinity softens the contours of his identity management efforts, which at other times seems rather strong (5:5; 6:5; 15:34–35).

POSSIBLE FUTURE SOCIAL IDENTITIES: LIFE BEYOND THIS LIFE (15:35–58)

In 15:35–44 Paul writes in the form of a debate to frame questions that likely would come to mind: "How are the dead raised? With what kind of body do they come?" He claims that such questions are foolish. He describes a seed that is planted and the plant that emerges (15:37; John 12:24; Tosefta *Sanhedrin* 90b). There is some continuity between the seed and the plant, but they are not completely identical. Paul is forming a future social identity that has some, but not complete, continuity between one's present existence and one's future life.

Paul goes on in 15:45–46 and picks up the earlier contrast between two prototypical figures associated with the Corinthians' in Christ social identity. He begins with an allusion to the Genesis story (Gen 2:7) and refers to

"Let All You Do Be Done in Love" (15:1—16:24)

"Adam" (15:45), rhetorically categorizing him as a member of the outgroup. Negative group prototypes reinforce members' understanding and experience of the ingroup and are central to accessing social memory.[4] In 15:22, Paul had noted that in "Adam all die." Thus, for Paul, an identity rooted in Adam is problematic since it is separate from the second Adam. Therefore, he reintroduces "the last Adam," Christ, who becomes, for Paul, the prototypical leader for the community. It is in Christ that one finds one's identity, one's future, and ultimately one's life. Paul has been writing an authorizing discourse seeking to transform significant aspects of Roman social identity, and in 15:46 he alludes to the fact that transformation is not optional.

Paul continues the comparison in 15:47–49 and notes the differing origins of the two prototypical figures: Adam is from the dust, and Christ is from heaven. He then makes the connection for his audience: earthly social identity (in Adam) is a non-transformed identity while a transformed identity is a heavenly identity (in Christ). The transformation does not preclude the continuity with the earthly identity already discussed (7:17–20). Yet Paul's rhetorical vision becomes clearer in 15:49 where he calls the Corinthian Christ-followers to "bear the image of the man from heaven," which is his goal for their transformed identity in Christ. Thus, "the image of the man of dust" is no longer primary. The social implications of Paul's argument come into focus: they need to reassess their affiliation and continued identification within the broader civic life in Corinth because they are now image-bearers of a holy God. The ongoing process of transformation in Christ has a central eschatological component that cannot be ignored but is fundamental; Paul uses it to form the identity narrative of the Christ-followers. It is hard to fully discern the

4. See Tucker, *Remain in Your Calling*, 224 n. 158.

eschatological problem in Corinth; it may be that Roman imperial eschatology had begun to impact their view of the future.

In 15:50–58, Paul again uses kinship language as a way to reinforce the ingroup identity. He points out that mere human identity is not enough to "inherit the kingdom of God" (15:50). He heightens the apocalyptic rhetoric by pointing out that his message is a "mystery" (15:51; 2:7). The term "mystery" does not indicate that his meaning is hidden; it points to a previously concealed truth that is now revealed (Rom 11:25). The specific mystery in this case is that "death" has been defeated (15:54–56) and that not all Christ-followers will "die." Some will be alive at the time of Christ's return (15:51–52; 1 Thess 4:15–17). Paul cites Isa 25:8 and Hos 13:14 to show that Christ has overcome death whose "sting" had come from "sin" and whose power had come from "the law" (Rom 7:4–20). For Paul, the law itself is not the problem (Rom 7:12); it is the sphere in which it operates that is crucial. Outside the sphere of Christ, the law has a negative function, but for those in Christ, particularly in light of Paul's eschatological perspective, it assumes a positive one (7:19; 9:21). Paul ends his description of this transformed future possible social identity by instructing his "beloved" to a new course of action. They are to "be steadfast, immoveable, always excelling in the work of the Lord" (15:58). When combined, these become indexes for a new shared identity, uniting the group since all that they do for the resurrected "Lord" will "not" be "in vain."

ECONOMIC SOCIAL IDENTITY: THE CULTIVATION OF GENEROSITY (16:1–4)

A transformed group ethos also emerges in new economic practices, since economic decisions are actually ones of

"Let All You Do Be Done in Love" (15:1—16:24)

identity. In 16:1–4, Paul seeks to form the economic aspects of the Corinthians' in Christ social identity by instructing them "concerning the collection for the saints." This is generally known as the Jerusalem collection (cf. Gal 2:10; 2 Cor 8:13–15; Rom 15:26). Paul offers different reasons for the collection based on the rhetorical context of each of these letters, but one aspect is consistent: he connects gentiles in Christ to God's covenant people, Israel. This passage in 1 Corinthians is one of Paul's earliest references to the collection and is also another example of the "now concerning" (*peri de*) formula which suggests that this issue was raised by the Corinthians themselves. Perhaps they were asking for clarification on the details of the project, or more likely some were interested in giving to the collection as a benefaction.[5] In the latter case, they would give to help Christ-followers in Jerusalem, and then expect that those in Jerusalem would, in turn, return honor and allegiance to them. This may be another example where patronage contributed to the malformation of an in Christ social identity among the Corinthians.

Paul uses the term "the collection" (*hē logeia*) in 16:1–2. This term generally referred to business documents such as tax reports, or money intended to be spent on rituals for various gods, e.g., the collection of Isis. Notably, this is the only place Paul uses this word. Elsewhere, he describes his financial project as "the service" (2 Cor 9:1) or "the partnership" (2 Cor 8:4), which both seem more in keeping with Paul's perspective on life within the Christ-movement. His use of *hē logeia* suggests that the Corinthians may have misunderstood "the collection" because of their socially embedded thinking about patronage. Paul, on the other hand, emphasizes mutuality and relationality. Further, since such collections were made to Isis, some of the Corinthians may

5. Tucker, "The Jerusalem Collection," 59–62.

have thought of Paul's collection as a type of benefaction directed to a provincial deity, a view equally problematic for Paul (12:2). In general, Paul works to transform the patronage system, which he likely refers to in 16:3 when he describes "your gift (*charis*) to Jerusalem," since the Greek word *charis* which underlies "gift" is taken from the patronage context. For Paul, God's "gift" transforms these one-way-oriented approaches into expressions of mutuality and economic flourishing marked by generosity. The Corinthians' participation will reveal the degree to which their in Christ identity is salient, and a later letter suggests that they eventually did contribute (Rom 15:26).

PARTNERSHIPS IN THE EARLIEST CHRIST-MOVEMENT (16:5–12)

Paul ends the letter with his travel plans and offers brief glimpses into the relational dynamics among Paul's partners in the gentile mission. He tells the Corinthians that after going from "Ephesus" to "Macedonia," he will return to Corinth. Unplanned changes to Paul's travel plans eventually contributed to the relational distance between him and the Corinthians (2 Cor 1:15–2:4, 1–11; 7:12). However, as of the writing of this letter he expected to spend a significant amount of time with them. Even in his mission to the nations, Paul still organizes his time around the Jewish calendar, noting that it is not yet "Pentecost" (16:8). This demonstrates that he has not, as is too often thought, left the ancestral traditions of Judaism behind and started a new religion, Christianity. The reference also suggests that his gentile addressees would have understood such a Jewish timekeeping reference, a conclusion that supports the thesis, mentioned in Chapters 1 and 6 of this book, that at

"Let All You Do Be Done in Love" (15:1—16:24)

this early date the community maintained its connections within the broader synagogue community.

One of Paul's key partners in this mission is "Timothy" (16:10). Often he is seen only as Paul's assistant; however, in 1 Thess 2:6, he is referred to as an "apostle" and in 2 Cor 1:19 he is described as one who "proclaimed" the gospel to the Corinthians. In 1 Corinthians, however, Timothy's main purpose was to embody the Christ-movement's halakic practices (4:17–21). It is unclear whether in fact Timothy ever arrived in Corinth. The word "if" and the Greek subjunctive verb in 16:10 suggest a sense of uncertainty about his trip. In addition, Paul seems clearly apprehensive about the way he will be received. He wants to make sure that Timothy will have nothing to "fear," that "no one will despise him," and that he will be allowed to leave again with the "brothers" in "peace" (16:11). This exchange highlights the tension between Paul and some of the Corinthians, but it also demonstrates that at this point in their relationship his leadership position is still salient. He still embodies the group's norms to the extent that he is able to encourage them towards a specific course of action, that they should treat "Timothy" as one who "is doing the work of the Lord" just as Paul is (16:10).

The final "now concerning" (*peri de*) occurs in 16:12; evidently the Corinthians had enquired into the whereabouts of "Apollos." As was mentioned earlier, some of the Corinthians were socially identifying with him as their ingroup prototype (1:12; 3:5–6, 22; 4:6). The relationship implied in 16:12 suggests again that there is no personal animosity between him and Paul. Furthermore, their association was such that Paul "urged him to visit," but "he was not at all willing to come." This reveals both a working relationship and Apollo's freedom to resist Paul's directive. Paul was only one among many leaders in the early

Christ-movement, and others, like Apollos, were negotiating their own identity in the context of their own calling to mission.

THE VISION FOR A TRANSFORMED ROMAN SOCIAL IDENTITY (16:13–18)

Paul closes the letter in 16:13–24 in a way that clarifies his main arguments in the previous chapters. His rhetorical vision, the shared group consciousness that he hopes to engender within the community, comes into focus. He has been seeking to transform key aspects of the Christ-followers' Roman social identity that have become problematic for the salience of their in Christ identity. His slightly gendered list of directives in 16:13, "keep alert, stand firm, be courageous, be strong," aligns closely with Roman expectations for masculinity and suggests again that Paul was not seeking to obliterate Roman social identity, only to transform it in Christ.[6]

Earlier in the letter Paul critiqued aspects of the Roman household structure. Now he uses the Roman household structure for his identity-forming program. The "household of Stephanas" is described through the resources of social memory; they were part of the original group of Christ-followers in "Achaia." This Roman household embodied "service" to "the saints," so Paul instructs the Corinthians to align themselves with them and "everyone who works and toils with them." Earlier in the letter, Paul mentioned that he "did baptize . . . the household of Stephanas" (1:16). By highlighting Paul's own relationship with them again in

---

6. Cobb, *Dying to be Men*, 146, cites the following: Cicero, *Tusculan Disputations*, 2.18.43; Plutarch, *Life of Coriolanus*, 1.6; Seneca, *Of Consolation to Helvia*, 16; Valerius Maximus, *Memorable Deeds and Sayings*, 7.6.1–3.

16:17, he is elevating them as prototypes of the pattern he wants the community to embody. Paul is not presenting a command-obedience structure, but a reminder of those who can guide the Christ-followers into maturity in Christ, in other words into a salient in Christ social identity. Paul wants the community to "give recognition to such persons" (16:18). The honor Paul gives to Stephanas's household embeds his rhetorical vision within the community and at the same time renews his own connection with them through their shared experience of being "refreshed" by this group of new old leaders (16:18).

EMERGENCE OF A SUPERORDINATE SOCIAL IDENTITY (16:19–20)

Another shared experience emerges again in the final verses, the sense of being in the Lord. This is not a vague feeling; it is embodied in the Corinthians' connections to Christ-followers outside of Corinth. Paul has worked throughout this letter to construct a trans-local identity for the Christ-followers, and he reminds them of it one last time by noting, "The churches of Asia send greetings." Paul is referring to those who are part of the Pauline Christ-movement in Ephesus and in other parts of the Roman province of Asia. He strengthens their connection more precisely when he mentions "Aquila and Prisca" who have a "church in their house." This couple had come into contact with Paul while in Corinth, and they later appear as leaders of a house church in Rome, which, as here, is described as an *ekklēsia* (Acts 18:2, 18, 26; Rom 16:3–5). The identity that all Christ-followers share, that Paul establishes as superordinate to all others, is not a theologically-bound, universalistic sense of belonging. Instead, Paul describes it in different ways depending on his rhetorical needs: in Christ, in the Lord, members of the body of Christ, or the Christ-group (*ekklēsia*). In this identity, there is an emerging sense of kinship, "brothers and sisters" who "send greetings," and an early form of ritual, a "holy kiss," which is part of a formative celebration that works against a universalistic understanding of identity (16:20).

PAUL'S LEADERSHIP IDENTITY, INFLUENCE, AND POWER (16:21–24)

Nestled at the end of this letter are a couple indicators of Paul's desire to form a new sense of "we" in the Corinthians. The identity-forming "holy kiss" just mentioned is contrasted with an explicit othering of the outgroup (16:22). This, along with the next phrase, an Aramaic expression, "our Lord, come" (*marana tha*), likely emerge from the worship setting of the earliest Christ-movement. They are part of a doxological social identity that Paul sought to form earlier. At the end of the letter, those inside the community that oppose Paul are othered (2 Cor 11:4) and the rest are reminded of the future orientation of an in-Christ social identity (11:26; 15:28). These two verses highlight Paul's leadership as one who influences others in a way that seeks to achieve the group's goals.

The final two verses offer a prayer that "the grace of the Lord Jesus be with you." This connects the end of the letter with the beginning, where his salutation included "grace to you" (1:3). God's gracious favor is more than an attitude; it is a social identification that emerges within a relationship and *not* some type of equity presupposed by the benefaction system, or a gift given to enhance one's social status. God's grace is relational and should result in an ethos of mutuality. In 16:21, "Paul" indicates he is "writing this greeting" himself but even after the formal conclusion

"Let All You Do Be Done in Love" (15:1—16:24)

in 16:23, he adds one more postscript, "my love be with all of you in Christ Jesus." This is the third time he mentions "love" at the end of the letter (16:14, 22, 24), and this, along with his earlier teaching (8:1–3; 13:1–13), suggests that love provides a crucial way of being in Christ and an alternative way of knowing in contrast to the wisdom of this world.

DISCUSSION QUESTIONS

1. Paul sought to form the identity of the Corinthians by emphasizing a future orientation to their identity in Christ. To what degree do you have this orientation? Why do you think Christ-followers today often resist discussions about the return of Christ? How would a renewed emphasis on the hope of Christ's return impact your daily life?

2. Different opinions concerning death were part of the problem in Corinth. How do differences on end of life issues adversely affect faith communities? How has the broader culture adversely affected you in relation to death? How do our discussions and practices relating to death reveal our Christian identity?

3. This chapter mentioned the idea of cultural translation difficulties. Can you think of ways our culture mishears the gospel? What would it mean for you to see yourself as a bicultural mediator? What would change in your life if you sought to embody Christ more than Adam? Are there any inherent gender limitations to Paul's argument?

4. Paul offers advice for the way the Corinthians should participate in the Jerusalem Collection. Why do you think financial support like this was crucial for these gentiles in Christ? If economic decisions are actually

identity ones, how does your Christian identity inform your economic practices? What is the contemporary relevance of the Jerusalem Collection? What values does it model that continue to be important?

5. After all the details Paul has covered, he concludes by saying, "Let everything you do be done in love." Why do you think that was his ultimate answer to their problems? Is relying on a principle of love the ultimate answer for our church disunity problems? If so, why do so few have it as their focus?

10

CONCLUSION

So what? Good professors always encourage students to ask this question. It challenges students to see the significance of the grammatical categories and should show them why they have put so much hard work into analyzing the text. Therefore, at the end of our study of 1 Corinthians, it is appropriate to ask, does it really matter if Paul was concerned with the formation of Roman social identity or the way existing identities continue in Christ? Should the Roman context of Corinth determine one's reading of the letter? Are the questions that social identity theory raises really the questions with which Paul wrestled? Do the gender, economic, or ethnic confusions of a small group of Christ-followers in ancient Greece have any implications for us at the start of the twenty-first century? Does thinking of Paul as an empowering leader rather than one who wielded his authority like a domineering Roman father change the way we form the identity of our churches today?

Yes, the answers to these questions do matter. Readers are ethically responsible for their interpretations. A person cannot simply say, "Don't blame me; this is just what Paul wrote." The questions Paul addressed are not so different from the questions we wrestle with in our own contemporary context: identity, authority, sexuality, marriage, gender orientation, cultural pluralism, worship differences, philosophical doubts, leadership disagreements, and economic inequality. So, yes, working hard to understand the social setting, rhetoric, and implications of the letter should help readers address similar topics where confusion over Christian identity and the social implications of the gospel are contributing to a lack of human flourishing (2:6; 14:20).[1]

This book has been concerned with Paul's theologizing in 1 Corinthians. It has demonstrated the way social identity theory, along with other considerations such as the persistence of Roman and Jewish identities in reprioritized ways, provides insight into the rhetorics of the text, especially about its social function. This alternative reading is designed to show the way Paul's argument contributed to the formation of social identity. Such an approach is likely to continue to provide useful insights for theology, especially if William S. Campbell is accurate in his claim that "identity precedes theology and that in fact theological constructions emerge to solve the problem of identity rather than create it."[2] In that case, the interface between the two is all the more important.

---

1. Tucker, "The Jerusalem Collection," 68, for a discussion of human flourishing as well-being.

2. Campbell, *Paul and the Creation*, 52.

Conclusion

DISCUSSION QUESTIONS

1. What contemporary deformations of Christian identity concern you? How can sustained theological reflection on 1 Corinthians assist in overcoming these problematic identity performances? How would asking the identity question before the theological one help in this endeavor?

2. Do you agree with the idea that you as a reader are ethically responsible for your interpretations of Scripture? Would any of your views have to change if you took this idea seriously? What interpretive principle from 1 Corinthians might guide contemporary readers when addressing ethical concerns not specifically dealt with in the letter?

BIBLIOGRAPHY

Adams, Edward, and David G. Horrell, eds. *Christianity at Corinth: The Quest for the Pauline Church.* Louisville: Westminster John Knox, 2004.

Ascough, Richard S. "Paul, Synagogues, and Associations: Reframing the Question of Models for Pauline Christ Groups." *Journal of the Jesus Movement in its Jewish Setting* 2 (2015) 27–52.

Bar-Tal, D. *Group Beliefs: A Conception for Analyzing Group Structure, Processes, and Behavior.* New York: Springer, 1990.

Barclay, John M. G. "1 Corinthians." In *The Oxford Bible Commentary*, edited by John Barton and John Muddiman, 1108–33. Oxford: Oxford University Press, 2001.

———. *Paul and the Gift.* Grand Rapids: Eerdmans, 2015.

Barentsen, Jack. *Emerging Leadership in the Pauline Mission: A Social Identity Perspective on Local Leadership Development in Corinth and Ephesus.* Eugene, OR: Pickwick, 2011.

Bartchy, Scott. "Paulus hat nicht gelehrt: 'Jeder soll in seinem Stand bleiben' Luthers Fehlübersetzung von *klēsis* in 1. Korinther 7." In *Alte Texte in neuen Kontexten: wo steht die sozialwissenschaftliche Exegese?*, edited by Wolfgang Stegeman and Richard DeMaris, 222–24. Stuttgart: Kohlhammer, 2010.

Bookidis, Nancy. "The Sanctuaries of Corinth." In *Corinth: The Centenary, 1896–1996*, edited by C. K. Williams II and Nancy Bookidis, 247–60. Athens: ASCSA, 2003.

Briones, David E. *Paul's Financial Policy: A Socio-Theological Approach.* London: Bloomsbury, 2013.

Campbell, William S. *Paul and the Creation of Christian Identity.* London: T. & T. Clark, 2006.

Ciampa, Roy E., and Brian S. Rosner. *The First Letter to the Corinthians.* Grand Rapids: Eerdmans, 2010.

Bibliography

Cinnirella, Marco. "Exploring Temporal Aspects of Social Identity: The Concept of Possible Social Identities." *European Journal of Social Psychology* 28 (1998) 227–48.

Clarke, Andrew. *Secular and Christian Leadership in Corinth*. Eugene, OR: Wipf and Stock, 2006.

Cobb, L. Stephanie. *Dying to Be Men: Gender and Language in Early Christian Martyr Texts*. New York: Columbia University Press, 2008.

Collins, Nathan. *All but Invisible: Exploring Identity Questions at the Intersection of Faith, Gender, and Sexuality*. Grand Rapids: Zondervan, 2017.

Coppins, Wayne. "To Eat or Not to Eat? Conversion, Bodily Practice, and the Relationship between Formal Worship and Everyday Life in the Anthropology of Religion and 1 Corinthians 8:7." *Biblical Theology Bulletin* 41 (2011) 84–91.

Ehrensperger, Kathy. *Paul and the Dynamics of Power: Communication and Interaction in the Early Christ-Movement*. London: T. & T. Clark, 2007.

———. *Paul at the Crossroads of Cultures: Theologizing in the Space-Between*. London: Bloomsbury, 2013.

Engels, Donald W. *Roman Corinth: An Alternative Model for the Classical City*. Chicago: University of Chicago Press, 1990.

Esler, Philip. *Conflict and Identity in Romans: The Social Setting of Paul's Letter*. Minneapolis: Fortress, 2003.

———. "An Outline of Social Identity Theory." In *T & T Clark Handbook to Social Identity in the New Testament*, edited by J. Brian Tucker and Coleman A. Baker, 13–39. London: Bloomsbury, 2014.

Fairclough, Norman. *Discourse and Social Change*. Cambridge: Polity, 1992.

Finney, Mark T. *Honour and Conflict in the Ancient World: 1 Corinthians in Its Greco-Roman Social Setting*. London: T. & T. Clark, 2012.

Fotopoulos, John. *Food Offered to Idols in Roman Corinth: A Social-Rhetorical Reconsideration of 1 Corinthians 8:1—11:1*. Tübingen: Mohr Siebeck, 2003.

Fredriksen, Paula. "The Question of Worship: Gods, Pagans, and the Redemption of Israel." In *Paul within Judaism: Restoring the First-Century Context to the Apostle*, edited by Mark D. Nanos and Magnus Zetterholm, 175–201. Minneapolis: Fortress, 2015.

Friesen, S. J. "Prospects for a Demography of the Pauline Mission: Corinth among the Churches." In *Urban Religion in Roman*

Bibliography

Corinth: Interdisciplinary Approaches, edited by D. Schowalter and S. Friesen, 352–70. Cambridge: Harvard University Press, 2005.

Furman, Richard. *Rev. Dr. Richard Furman's Exposition of the Views of the Baptists, Relative to the Coloured Population of the United States, in a Communication to the Governor of South-Carolina*. Charleston: A. E. Miller, 1823.

Goodrich, John. *Paul as an Administrator of God in 1 Corinthians*. New York: Cambridge University Press, 2012.

Harrill, J. A. *The Manumission of Slaves in Early Christianity*. Hermeneutische Untersuchungen zur Theologie 32. Tübingen: J. C. B. Mohr (Paul Siebeck), 1995.

Haslam, S. Alexander, Stephen Reicher, and Michael Platow. *The New Psychology of Leadership: Identity, Influence, and Power*. Hove: Psychology, 2011.

Hinkle, S., and R. Brown. "Intergroup Comparisons and Social Identity: Some Links and Lacunae." In *Social Identity Theory: Constructive and Critical Advances*, edited by D. Abrams and M. A. Hogg, 48–70. New York: Springer, 1990.

Ho, Sin-Pan Daniel, *Paul and the Creation of a Counter-Cultural Community: A Rhetorical Analysis of 1 Cor. 5.1—11.1 in Light of the Social Lives of the Corinthians*. London: Bloomsbury, 2015.

Hogg, M. A., and D. Abrams, *Social Identifications: A Social Psychology of Intergroup Relations and Group Processes*. London: Routledge, 1988.

Hunt, Laura J. *The Not-Very-Persecuted Church: Paul at the Intersection of Church and Culture*. Eugene, OR: Resource, 2011.

Kent, J. H. *The Inscriptions, 1926–1950*. Princeton, NJ: ASCSA, 1966.

Levine, Amy-Jill, and Marc Zvi Brettler. *The Jewish Annotated New Testament: New Revised Standard Version Bible Translation*. Oxford: Oxford University Press, 2011.

Malcolm, Matthew R. *World of 1 Corinthians: An Exegetical Source Book of Literary and Visual Backgrounds*. Eugene, OR: Cascade, 2013.

Malina, Bruce J. *The New Testament World: Insights from Cultural Anthropology*. Louisville: Westminster John Knox, 2001.

May, Alistair Scott. *"The Body for the Lord": Sex and Identity in 1 Corinthians 5–7*. JSNTSup 278. London: T. & T. Clark, 2004.

Millis, Benjamin W. "The Local Magistrates and Elite of Roman Corinth." In *Corinth in Contrasts: Studies in Inequality*, edited by Steven J. Friesen, Sarah A. James, and Daniel N. Schowalter, 38–53. Leiden: Brill, 2014.

Bibliography

Nanos, Mark D. "Paul and Judaism: Why Not Paul's Judaism?" In *Paul Unbound: Other Perspectives on the Apostle*, edited by Mark D. Given, 117–60. Peabody: Hendrickson, 2010.

Nanos, Mark D., and Magnus Zetterholm, eds. *Paul within Judaism: Restoring the First-Century Context to the Apostle*. Minneapolis: Fortress, 2015.

Peppiatt, Lucy. *Women and Worship at Corinth: Paul's Rhetorical Arguments in 1 Corinthians*. Eugene, OR: Cascade, 2015.

Rudolph, David J. *A Jew to the Jews: Jewish Contours of Pauline Flexibility in 1 Corinthians 9.19–23*. 2nd ed. Eugene, OR: Pickwick, 2016.

Starling, David I. *UnCorinthian Leadership: Thematic Reflections on 1 Corinthians*. Eugene, OR: Cascade, 2014.

Tajfel, H. *Human Groups and Social Categories: Studies in Social Psychology*. Cambridge: Cambridge University Press, 1981.

———. "Interindividual Behaviour and Intergroup Behaviour." In *Differentiation between Social Groups: Studies in the Social Psychology of Intergroup Relations*, edited by H. Tajfel, 27–60. London: Academic, 1978.

———. "Social Categorization, Social Identity and Social Comparison." In *Differentiation between Social Groups: Studies in the Social Psychology of Intergroup Relations*, edited by H. Tajfel, 61–76. London: Academic, 1978.

Tomson, Peter J. *Paul and the Jewish Law: Halakha in the Letters of the Apostle to the Gentiles*. Minneapolis: Fortress, 1990.

Tucker, J. Brian. "The Jerusalem Collection, Economic Inequality, and Human Flourishing: Is Paul's Concern the Redistribution of Wealth, or a Relationship of Mutuality (or Both)?" *Canadian Theological Review* 3 (2014) 52–70.

———. "Religious Leaders: New Testament." In *The Oxford Encyclopedia of the Bible and Gender Studies*, edited by Julia M. O'Brien, 184–89. New York: Oxford University Press, 2014.

———. *Remain in Your Calling: Paul and the Continuation of Social Identities in 1 Corinthians*. Eugene, OR: Pickwick, 2011.

———. *You Belong to Christ: Paul and the Formation of Social Identity in 1 Corinthians 1–4*. Eugene, OR: Pickwick, 2010.

Tucker, J. Brian, and Coleman A. Baker, eds. *T & T Clark Handbook to Social Identity in the New Testament*. London: Bloomsbury, 2014.

Turner, J. C. "The Experimental Social Psychology of Intergroup Behavior." In *Intergroup Behavior*, edited by J. C. Turner and H. Giles, 66–101. Oxford: Blackwell, 1981.

Bibliography

Van der Watt, J. G., ed. *Identity, Ethics, and Ethos in the New Testament.* Beihefte zur Zeitschrift für die neutestamentliche Wissenschaft 141. Berlin: de Gruyter, 2006.

Welborn, L. L. *Paul, the Fool of Christ: A Study of 1 Corinthians 1–4 in the Comic-Philosophic Tradition.* London: T. & T. Clark, 2005.

Westfall, Cynthia Long. *Paul and Gender: Reclaiming the Apostle's Vision for Men and Women in Christ.* Grand Rapids: Baker, 2016.

Witherington, Ben III. *Conflict and Community in Corinth: A Socio-Rhetorical Commentary on 1 and 2 Corinthians.* Grand Rapids: Eerdmans, 1995.

Wolter, M. "'Let No One Seek His Own, but Each One the Other's' (1 Corinthians 10, 24): Pauline Ethics According to 1 Corinthians." In *Identity, Ethics, and Ethos in the New Testament*, edited by J. G. van der Watt, 199–217. Beihefte zur Zeitschrift für die neutestamentliche Wissenschaft 141. Berlin: Walter de Gruyter, 2006.

www.ingramcontent.com/pod-product-compliance
Lightning Source LLC
Chambersburg PA
CBHW020830190426
43197CB00037B/1107